LUKAS & STERNBERG, NEW YORK 010

CERITH WYN EVANS
"CERITH WYN EVANS"

SCHOOL OF THE MUSEUM OF FINE ARTS
AT TUFTS UNIVERSITY

LUKAS & STERNBERG, NEW YORK

Cerith Wyn Evans

"Cerith Wyn Evans"

Publisher/Verlag: Lukas & Sternberg, New York

© 2004 Cerith Wyn Evans, Frankfurter Kunstverein, Lukas & Sternberg, the authors and photographers/
die Autoren und Fotografen

All rights reserved, including the right of reproduction in whole or in part in any form.

Exhibition/Ausstellung: Frankfurter Kunstverein, March 31 – May 23, 2004

Supported by/mit freundlicher Unterstützung von: British Council and/und DekaBank

..DekaBank

Partner des Frankfurter Kunstvereins

Editor/Herausgeber: Daniel Buchholz, Christopher Müller, Nicolaus Schafhausen

Editing and proofreading/Redaktion und Lektorat: Vanessa Joan Müller

Translation/Übersetzung: Fiona Elliott, Manfred Hermes, Steven Lindberg

Design/Gestaltung: Sandra Kastl, Markus Weisbeck, surface, Berlin/Frankfurt am Main

Printing and binding/Druck und Bindung: Medialis, Berlin

ISBN: 0-9745688-1-3

Lukas & Sternberg

Caroline Schneider

1182 Broadway #1602, New York NY 10001

Linienstraße 159, D-10115 Berlin

mail@lukas-sternberg.com, www.lukas-sternberg.com

CONTENTS / INHALT

ANDREAS SPIEGL
A SHORT AESTHETICS OF KNOWLEDGE   11
EINE KLEINE ÄSTHETIK DES WISSENS   29

JAN VERWOERT
AT NIGHT THEY TALK TO EACH OTHER ON THE RADIO   41
NACHTS SPRECHEN SIE MITEINANDER IM RADIO   63

JULIANE REBENTISCH
DECOLONIZED THEATER   81
DAS ENTKOLONISIERTE THEATER   109

MANFRED HERMES
THIS DOUBLE GROUND OF SPACE: TEXT, TRANSLATION, AND BREATHING – INTERVIEW WITH CERITH WYN EVANS   125
DIESE DOPPELBÖDIGKEIT DES RAUMS: TEXT, ÜBERSETZUNG, ATMEN – INTERVIEW MIT CERITH WYN EVANS   147

BIOGRAPHY / BIOGRAFIE   161

EXHIBITIONS / AUSSTELLUNGEN   163

THE DANGERS OF TAKING PLEASURE IN THE PAST AND THE BENEFITS OF REMEMBERING IN ORDER TO REINVENT ARE NOT CLEARLY POSTED. THERE IS A RISK OF PEDDLING NOSTALGIA, OF GETTING LOST AND/OR PARALYSED IN EMOTIONALLY INFLECTED TERRITORY IN WHICH RECREATION OF THE PAST OBSCURES AND REPLACES (OR DISPLACES) THE PRESENT. TO AID CRITICAL UNDERSTANDING OF PAST SPECIFICITIES, AND THEIR EFFECT IN THE PRESENT, IT SEEMS MORE PRODUCTIVE TO CONSIDER LOOSE CONTINUUMS OF PRODUCTION THAN TO PROVIDE A FORM OF PERIODIZATION AS PUNCTUATION.

HOW TO BALANCE MULTIPLE RELATIONS TO HISTORY? ALTERNATIVES TO TRADITIONAL HISTORIOGRAPHIC PRACTISES MIGHT TRACE SPATIAL AND TEMPORAL CONFIGURATIONS OF INTERCONNECTED EVENTS, ACTIVITIES, AND ASSOCIATIONS OF IDEAS NESTED IN CULTURAL CIRCUMSTANCES, AND BY DESIGN PROVIDE SPACES FOR MULTIPLE MEANINGS, CONFLICTING IMAGINATIONS, CONFLICTING "FACTS" AND PARTIALITY. HISTORIOGRAPHY MIGHT BE APPROACHED AKIN TO ARTISTIC METHODOLOGIES, UTILIZE JUXTAPOSITION AND ARTISTIC LICENSE, RENDER AMBIVALENTLY RATHER THAN DECLARATIVELY, AND ULTIMATELY ACKNOWLEDGE, NOT ONLY IN PRINCIPLE BUT AS PART OF A HISTORICIZING METHOD ITSELF, THAT HISTORIOGRAPHY IS A CREATIVE AS WELL AS AN INTERPRETIVE PRACTICE: THAT IT IS A FORM OF PRODUCTION.

(JULIE AULT, *THE DOUBLE EDGE OF HISTORY*)

DIE MOMENTE, IN DENEN MAN GEFAHR LÄUFT, SICH AN DER VERGANGENHEIT ZU ERGÖTZEN, SIND SCHWER VON JENEN ZU TRENNEN, IN DENEN MAN AUS DER ERINNERUNG NEUES ZU SCHÖPFEN BEGINNT. ES BESTEHT IMMER DIE GEFAHR, IN NOSTALGIE ZU VERFALLEN ODER SICH AUF EMOTIONAL VERBRÄMTEN TERRAIN ZU VERIRREN (BZW. SICH DAVON FESSELN ZU LASSEN), WO DIE REKONSTRUKTION DER VERGANGENHEIT DIE GEGENWART ÜBERSCHATTET ODER GANZ VERDRÄNGT. UM EIN KRITISCHES VERSTÄNDNIS VON HISTORISCHEN BESONDERHEITEN UND DEREN AUSWIRKUNGEN AUF DIE GEGENWART ZU FÖRDERN, SCHEINT ES ZIELFÜHRENDER, PRODUKTIONSPROZESSE IN LOSEN KONTINUIERLICHEN ZEITRÄUMEN ZU BETRACHTEN, ALS DABEI NACH STRENGEN PERIODISIERUNGEN VORZUGEHEN.

WIE KANN EINE GESCHICHTSSCHREIBUNG AUSSEHEN, DIE VIELFÄLTIGE HERANGEHENSWEISEN AN DIE VERGANGENHEIT BERÜCKSICHTIGT? ALTERNATIVEN ZUR TRADITIONELLEN HISTORIOGRAPHIE HABEN VIELLEICHT AM EHESTEN EINE CHANCE, DIE RÄUMLICHEN UND ZEITLICHEN KONFIGURATIONEN INEINANDER VERWOBENER EREIGNISSE, AKTIVITÄTEN UND IDEENKETTEN NACHZUZEICHNEN, DURCH DIE SICH KULTURELLE ZUSAMMENHÄNGE HERAUSBILDEN, UND BEWUSST EINEN RAUM FÜR UNTERSCHIEDLICHE BEDEUTUNGEN, KONTROVERSE VORSTELLUNGEN, WIDERSPRÜCHLICHE „SACHVERHALTE" UND PARTEIISCHE PERSPEKTIVEN ZU ERÖFFNEN. MAN SOLLTE SICH DER GESCHICHTSSCHREIBUNG NÄHERN WIE KÜNSTLERISCHEN VORGEHENSWEISEN; GEGENÜBERSTELLUNGEN VERWENDEN UND KÜNSTLERISCHE FREIHEITEN NUTZEN; DIE DINGE EHER AMBIVALENT ALS DEKLARIEREND WIEDERGEBEN; UND ZU GUTER LETZT SOLLTE MAN SICH – NICHT NUR PRINZIPIELL, SONDERN IM BEZUG AUF DIE HISTORIOGRAPHISCHE METHODE SELBST – EINGESTEHEN, DASS DIE GESCHICHTSSCHREIBUNG EINE KREATIVE WIE AUCH INTERPRETIERENDE TÄTIGKEIT IST, KURZUM: EINE FORM VON PRODUKTION.

(JULIE AULT, *DIE ZWEISCHNEIDIGKEIT DER GESCHICHTE*)

ANDREAS SPIEGL
A SHORT AESTHETICS OF KNOWLEDGE

ARMANDO BALLESTER: TO WHAT EXTENT DO YOU THINK FILM IS A COMPLETELY INDEPENDENT MEDIUM FROM THE OTHERS?

JEAN-LUC GODARD: IT'S BOTH. IT IS COMPLETELY INDEPENDENT, AND IT BELONGS TO ALL THE OTHERS.

ARMANDO BALLESTER: COULD YOU EXPLAIN THAT?

JEAN-LUC GODARD: I'M AFRAID NOT. IT'S A FEELING, AND I CAN'T EXPLAIN IT. NO – AS A MATTER OF FACT, IT'S NOT A FEELING; IT'S A FACT. BUT I CAN'T EXPLAIN IT.[01]

AUDIENCE: IT SEEMS THAT YOUR FILMS ARE GROWING MORE AND MORE ABSTRACT; I WONDER IF YOU COULD EXPLAIN ...

JEAN-LUC GODARD: I'M SORRY, I CAN'T ANSWER THE QUESTION BECAUSE I SEE NO DIFFERENCE BETWEEN THE CONCRETE AND THE ABSTRACT.[02]

AUDIENCE: WHAT DO YOU THINK ABOUT THE DIFFERENCES BETWEEN THEATER AND MOVIES?

JEAN-LUC GODARD: I SEE NO DIFFERENCE BETWEEN THEATER AND MOVIES. IT IS ALL THEATER. IT IS SIMPLY A MATTER OF UNDERSTANDING WHAT THEATER MEANS.[03]

In accepting the invitation to write a text about the work of an artist who himself draws on a multiplicity of texts and diverse authors, one might be tempted to take his output as a sequence of building blocks which – according to the principle of cause and effect – only need to be added together in order for one to understand the ultimate message. The quotations and references would be the source of the causal factors – named by Cerith Wyn Evans – from which he derives his own questions and extrapolations; this in turn would explain his perspectives on reality and hence his work. Without wishing to pre-empt the conclusion: were one to attempt to create the architecture of an argument from the combined thinking of Theodor W. Adorno, John Cage, Jean-Luc Godard, William Burroughs, Guy Debord, Terry Wilson and Brion Gysin with Madame de Lafayette, Eve Kosofsky Sedgwick,

---

[01] JEAN-LUC GODARD, *INTERVIEWS*, ED. BY DAVID STERRIT (UNIVERSITY PRESS OF MISSISSIPPI, 1998), 41.

[02] IBID., 14.

[03] IBID.

Pier Paolo Pasolini, Bertolt Brecht, Luigi Pirandello, Samuel Morse and Judith Butler the end-result would closely resemble the Tower of Babel – an argumentative construction site for all time and yet, a manifesto of the irrational which triumphs over the rational and "common knowledge".

Looking more closely at the different authors and references in Cerith Wyn Evans's work, it is clear that their very difference does not serve to apostrophise the irrational as proof of the limits of the rational but lays bare the ideological and political core of irrational rationality. The deciphering of polyphonic messages is less about understanding an undisclosed text than about describing the effects of this irrational rationality, which might more simply be termed "common sense". As such the works of Cerith Wyn Evans are about the effects of a social contract which conceals the irrational power relation between people and cultures by explaining it and elucidating it – as the effect that follows a cause. If the references and texts that Cerith Wyn Evans draws on do have an element in common – for all their heterogeneity – then it is this suspicion of the rationalisation of the irrational which is supposed to be concealed and veiled. Against this backdrop, any analysis trying to unearth the foundations of the work will find itself in crisis because it is itself in danger – as it reconstructs those foundations – of coming up with an argument for reality which (in view of its political and social effects) is itself already in crisis. [The German *Grund*, translated here as "foundations", usefully implies both "foundations" and "reason", as in English "grounds".] Instead of explaining the effects by constructing a causal foundation, Cerith Wyn Evans's works engage in an analysis of the effects.

Unlike the causes, the effects come across as perceptible phenomena. They are not hidden from sight, but lie on the surface of things. Effects are phenomena that may have lost their foundations [*Grund*] or which never had any foundations. Because these effects do constitute perceptible phenomena they are of the present – regardless of how far back the causes lie. The presentness of effects therefore generates a specific relationship to history. What can be allocated to different historical epochs and separated chronologically retreats from the perspective of effects and enters a phase of synchrony – a simultaneous "still". When Cerith Wyn Evans draws on a novel written by Madame de Lafayette in 1678, this is because – despite its historical aspect – this text "still" poses questions that he can relate to those of other authors and later times. Despite their historical variables, by their effect they generate a virulent present. This virulent present acknowledges in the works not only the contents, which explain and seek to be understood, but also a performative quality, which consists in the fact that the works are still (and once again) in the position to have an effect on the perception of the present – even when they cannot be understood. In that sense their effect has an irrational component that one can understand without knowing on what it is founded.

Cerith Wyn Evans has spoken in various interviews of his first visit to Tokyo. Having been given a room high up in a skyscraper he looked out of the window and viewed the huge sea of flickering lights, ...
"I thought, if only I could tune in to what the city was saying, then there would be this vast, dense, polyphony of texts that are all somehow speaking at the same time, all over-riding each other, all reading at different speeds, that somehow ... the city became this vast coded text. I was very interested in the notion of something being in code."[04]
Wyn Evans identifies the city as a text asking to be decoded but which does not have to be decoded. The sea of lights seems to him like a text whose contents cannot be understood or deciphered – and yet the impression is as though its meaning had been decoded: the performative quality of a text that is effective and eloquent without having to say anything. What Cerith Wyn Evans is describing through this impression is a language that appears purely in its languageness, as unalloyed language, as *langue*. It is not important what it says but that

04 CERITH WYN EVANS, *LOOK AT THAT PICTURE* ... ; WHITE CUBE, LONDON 2003.

it can say something – that it works as language, holding a channel of communication open.

Given that Cerith Wyn Evans draws on a variety of texts and authors and integrates these into his work, the question arises as to whether his works are supposed to be decoded, by a process of analysing and understanding these references. However, if the point were solely this hermeneutic undertaking, then another question would still remain unanswered: Why does Wyn Evans translate these texts into a language based on Morse code which is itself distinctly dated? New information technology has taken over from Morse code which, as a consequence, barely anyone can understand nowadays. Since we are hardly likely to accuse the artist of codifying his texts simply in order to imbue his work with the aura of a secret message, the answer must be sought elsewhere.

Morse code, developed by the American painter and inventor Samuel Morse in the early 19th century when Modernity was in its infancy, uses a system of dots and dashes which can be transmitted as light signals or sound, visually or acoustically. This binary system recalls both the translation of numbers into sequences of 0 and 1 (going back to Leibniz) and the modern, Impressionist analysis of perception which puts the neurological message before the meaning of the painting. In other words, before the brain recognises the image, the eye merely perceives meaningless impulses, which will only add up to colours, forms and the relevant meanings through interpretation. By analogy, the contents of Wyn Evans's message will remain hidden from anyone who is not familiar with the relationship of the dots and dashes to letters. But even if the message is not understood, nevertheless one does have the impression that this is a language. One can recognise from the light signals transmitted here that this is simply an unfamiliar language which, because of its incomprehensibility, appears as pure languageness: not as a secret seeking to be decoded but as a picture of language, as *langue*. The flickering lights of the chandeliers which transmit texts in Morse code tell of a language that communicates independent of its contents – like the sea of lights extending across Tokyo which cannot be deciphered yet which signals the essence of language.

Transmitted as Morse code, the texts are not primarily translated as contents but as writing. Letter for letter, as dots and dashes, the texts in the lights of the chandeliers appear as writing again. One's desire to read and understand the texts is fulfilled by computer screens. The chandeliers fulfil a different function. Although serving the texts, they are specifically concerned with the writing: with writing as a process that generates meaning – in other words: the performative energy that is intrinsic to language. Language is not treated here as a vessel that contains something, but as a force that is in the position to generate something, even if this be an abstract channel of communication. Written letters and writing are not regarded as a technique for formulating a thought but as a path which opens up room for thought even in the process of writing. And what applies to writing, also applies to reading. Letter for letter, meaning evolves which generates a body of contents as a performative figure. From this perspective the attempt to decipher the lost system of Morse code leads to a notion of reading which cannot separate the contents from the adventure and the spectacle that went with the first experience of reading, combining letters and words into interconnected meanings: the experience of language as a place of pledges, as a message, as the promise of meaning.

In so far as we are talking here of writing, texts and language, then it is in the same sense that underpinned the development of Morse code: the variability of the medium through which language can articulate itself. As we have already said, the system of dots and dashes can be used to transmit the letters as visual, acoustic or electric signals. The appearance of language may vary: a text, translated into sound, may resonate at different pitches like a piece of music – and, translated into light signals, captured on celluloid, it may look like a Structuralist film. If the light impulses illuminate a space, like Cerith

Wyn Evans's chandeliers, then the text in translation appears like a *mise en scène* – a linguistic zone which promises that whatever occurs in this space will be perceived in the light of a particular meaning, will even be cast in an epistemological glow.

The Enlightenment, it should not be forgotten – linking cognition and knowledge [*Erkenntnis*] with the metaphor of light – grew from the idea that, in the light of rationalism, judgements could be observed and objectivised, in the same sense that photography captures the moment. Associated with this aesthetic of objectivisability was a notion of language that was in the position to formulate and capture a cognitive insight: the sentence as a snapshot of a thought which – in the light of rationalism – is no longer purely a performative figure, but which turns into the identifiable foundations and point of departure for the next thought and the next, which as a sequence, establish a reserve of knowledge – as knowledge that can multiply without affecting its core meaning. This knowledge in the age of its scientific and methodical reproducibility relies on the notion that it can mediate a thought independent of the cultural-historical context of the human subject. If the thought is valid for one subject, then it has enlightenment value for all others. This subject in search of enlightenment is duty-bound to perceive that knowledge as a reproducible entity. The paradoxical nature of this undertaking – paying homage to the enlightened subject even as it becomes lost in its own reproducibility was characteristic of the contradiction of Modernity in the 19th century. If photography – invented at almost exactly the same time as Morse came up with his code – was a medium which, like rational thought, could objectively capture reality in the light of its appearance, then it was film which – despite its reproducibility – was inextricably caught up in the present of its projection and the immediate effect on the viewing subject. Just as the reading subject has to follow the writing letter for letter, film demands a form of perception from the subject that is related to the act of reading. Word for word, image for image, meanings emerge which are as impossible to pin down as the notion of "the subject". While film in the late 19th century already highlighted the impossibility of the cognising subject pinning down or "fixing" a certain perception, Oscar Wilde for one told a parallel tale in his contemporaneous *Portrait of Dorian Gray*. The "fixable" subject, the fixable picture of the subject and the idea of fixable knowledge fail because of a language that wants to fix or pin down a particular notion of reality – thereby not recognising the performative act of speaking, reading or perceiving.

Film insists on precisely this activity of perception. You can only follow it if you follow it. Unlike photography, which captures the moment, film sweeps the subject along with it. If we wanted to extend the metaphor of light to this cognitive insight [*Erkenntnis*], one might say that film provides the light for such insights in Modernity. This light is neither a constant nor a metaphysical force that hauls the truth out into the light and enlighteningly illuminates it, but a mobile, constantly changing figure: reproducible yet inscribed into the being of change and into the moment – closer to writing than to the text. In the context of film, the text for the film is only thinkable as part of the "book". The German *Drehbuch* ["drehen" originally means "to turn"] for film script, evokes the "rolling" of the camera as the "book" is set in motion. In English the word "script" attributes the same significance to the writing, the act of writing, and the final text. However much a book or a text has a certain content, from the perspective of Modernity these contents are beholden to the moment of reading. What seems fixed and reproducible, always appears in one's perception as a changeable dimension. Unlike the Enlightenment, the cognitive insights of Modernity do not lead to the progressive self-consolidation of the subject, but to the fact that the cognitive subject changes itself through cognition. Mallarmé's opening up of the text as a piece of writing that can be read and understood differently again and again and again seems all too legitimate in the concurrent light of the first film projectors.

Although Cerith Wyn Evans has chosen to use Modernist chandeliers to inscribe his Morse encoded "scripts" into the present, again and again, each time anew, the texts he is drawing on appear in a filmic perspective. For although these chandeliers do look like chandeliers, the light they emit is related to the flickering light of the film projector. The adaptability of Morse code allows Evans to turn these texts into "scripts". Independently of their historical embeddedness, they flicker in the present of their projection; they promise a languageness that is no longer able to separate the contents from their perception by a subject which – whether looking or reading – always mutates in some way during the act of perception. The texts translated into scripts transform the subject itself – in the flickering light – into a varying figure. "Enlightened", the subject finds him/herself in a *mise en scène*. As variably as Morse code can be transmitted, the same variability is seen when the translated text appears as a film, a drama or a script. What may be interpreted at first sight as an installation, turns out on a second viewing to be a film, on the third it is clearly a drama and by the fourth it has become a reading room. The question as to the role of the subject in this *mise en scène* is determined by the particular perspective of that subject. Cerith Wyn Evans has already signalled an interest in this variability of the subject's role in another interview. He talks "enthusiastically" about a scene in Jean-Luc Godard's *Two Or Three Things I Know About Her* (1966): Godard films the actress Marina Vlady (playing the part of Juliette Jeanson) twice with the same camera angle, performing the same action on a balcony against the backdrop of the city. During the first shot the voice-over tells us, "Now we are seeing the actress Marina Vlady, she is of Russian origin, she's looking to the left … ", during the second shot it tells us, "Now we are seeing Juliette Jeanson … ".[05] The same person, the same place, the same action, and yet there is a considerable shift within the reproduction which conceives the subject in different roles.

The idea of associating light – seen from the perspective of film – with a concept of reality which in reality itself turns out to be a projective,

---

[05] CF. HANS ULRICH OBRIST, *INTERVIEWS* (CERITH WYN EVANS), VOL. 1 (ART PUB. INC., MILANO, 2003), 942F.

varying figure, has already featured in other works by Cerith Wyn Evans. In *Has the film already started* (2000) Wyn Evans – you might say – translates film back into light. Wyn Evans "re-filmed" Gil Wolman's *L'Anti-Concept*, by taking a camera and filming the light directly as it came out of the projector lens. The result is a film which consists of flickering light – an analogy to the filmed film – but with no recognisable motifs, apart from the central motif of the changing light. This light is projected onto a balloon floating in the space; despite its physicality and three-dimensionality the balloon fulfils the function of a projection surface. What was conceived as a film entitled *L'Anti-Concept*, is – contrary to its concept – transposed back into a filmic space, which now looks like a reality that changes as the light changes and as one walks around in it: a theatrical reality, a reality of stage-direction which retains a documentary, realistic connection with the question "what is film?". Jean-Luc Godard who, like Wyn Evans, responds to this question by alluding to Brecht and to Pirandello's *Six Characters in Search of an Author*, has this answer: " ... to show the common ground between realism and theatricality. Each has its separate frontier but there are certain points at which they merge."[06]

In other works by Cerith Wyn Evans, the suture between film, theatre and reality is marked by a fluorescent sign [in German "light script"] mounted on the wall – as though it were the subtitle of a lost film which has left only a filmic subtext for the perception of reality. The filmic subtitle transforms reality into a film, only the images have been withheld so imagined images can make way for reality. While one subtext reads "meanwhile ... across town", possibly evoking Cerith Wyn Evans's view from his Tokyo hotel room with the flickering city looking like a monumental film on endless quantities of text, another strip of

---

[06] JEAN-LUC GODARD, *INTERVIEWS*, ED. BY DAVID STERRIT, UNIVERSITY PRESS OF MISSISSIPPI, 1998, P. 5. CF. CERITH WYN EVANS'S DESCRIPTION OF A CHANDELIER IN AN INTERVIEW: "IT'S A MODERNIST, CLASSIC STEP BACK, A BRECHTIAN STEP BACK. IT'S THE SAME STEP THAT PIRANDELLO TAKES IN *SIX CHARACTERS IN SEARCH OF AN AUTHOR.*" IN: CERITH WYN EVANS: *LOOK AT THAT PICTURE...* ; WHITE CUBE, LONDON 2003.

illuminated writing in the form of a Möbius ring (1997) marks the never ceasing transformation and reversal of inside and outside, script and form, movement and repetition, drama and reality, film and theatre, which at certain moments merge into each other.

Cerith Wyn Evans's work with light as his medium allows him to connect diverse media and genres. The translation of texts into light signals and the transformation of films back into "light pictures" on one hand, and the three-dimensional *mise en scène* of writing as fluorescent signs on the other hand, generate multi-lingual, multi-vocal spaces that refer to film and theatre as much as to literature and theory. Although particular mention has not been made here of the music and the sound in Cerith Wyn Evans's works, nevertheless it still seems fair to refer to them collectively as a polyphonic light concert. The use of light as an integrative medium, which allows an author to turn scripts, texts and films into a spatial, theatrical event suggests a metaphor of cognitive insight bound up in momentariness and in the present. This light draws all the references contained within it into a concertante situation, which gives every exhibition the character of a dramatic performance. This character is what gives the cited, translated and implicit knowledge expressed in the various works a role suited to the contemporary notion of the subject. This knowledge is not a progressively growing architecture of insights which only need to be combined and which are connected to some future, unattainable ideal; this knowledge, affective and temporary in nature, is directed towards a subject and his/her political and discursive present – incapable of distancing him/herself, affected by the effects of the heterogeneous appearances of reality and knowing his/her own role which consists of playing several roles, without being able to understand what caused them. Foucault once outlined an "archaeology of knowledge"; Evans responds with an aesthetic of knowledge that has exchanged the old light of enlightenment for the filmic light of projection. This knowledge does not operate on the basis of common sense according to which there is agreement as to a common cause and its effects, but in its own presentness, which only lights up in the flickering attention of the subject. As the works thrive on light, so knowing thrives on the projection of knowledge.

TRANSLATED FROM THE GERMAN BY FIONA ELIOTT.

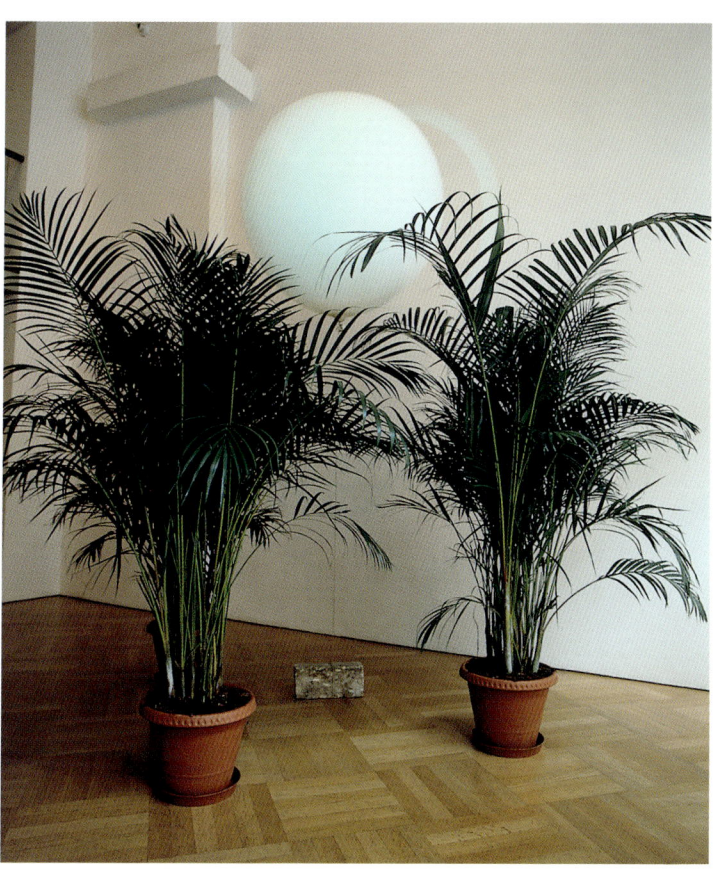

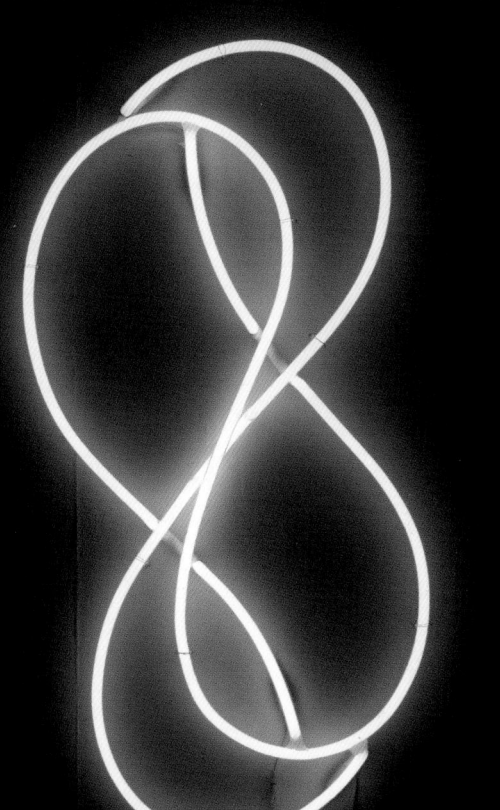

Has the film already started?, 2000
DVD, projector, CD, CD player, helium balloons, brick and string and plants
Dimensions variable

Meanwhile ... across town, 2001
Neon, 9 x 120,2 x 5 cm

Moebius Strip, 1997
Neon, 100 x 50 cm

ANDREAS SPIEGL
EINE KLEINE ÄSTHETIK DES WISSENS

ARMANDO BALLESTER: TO WHAT EXTENT DO YOU THINK FILM IS A COMPLETELY INDEPENDENT MEDIUM FROM THE OTHERS?
JEAN-LUC GODARD: IT'S BOTH. IT IS COMPLETELY INDEPENDENT, AND IT BELONGS TO ALL THE OTHERS.
ARMANDO BALLESTER: COULD YOU EXPLAIN THAT?
JEAN-LUC GODARD: I'M AFRAID NOT. IT'S A FEELING, AND I CAN'T EXPLAIN IT. NO – AS A MATTER OF FACT, IT'S NOT A FEELING; IT'S A FACT. BUT I CAN'T EXPLAIN IT.[01]

AUDIENCE: IT SEEMS THAT YOUR FILMS ARE GROWING MORE AND MORE ABSTRACT; I WONDER IF YOU COULD EXPLAIN ...
JEAN-LUC GODARD: I'M SORRY, I CAN'T ANSWER THE QUESTION BECAUSE I SEE NO DIFFERENCE BETWEEN THE CONCRETE AND THE ABSTRACT.[02]

AUDIENCE: WHAT DO YOU THINK ABOUT THE DIFFERENCES BETWEEN THEATER AND MOVIES?
JEAN-LUC GODARD: I SEE NO DIFFERENCE BETWEEN THEATER AND MOVIES. IT IS ALL THEATER. IT IS SIMPLY A MATTER OF UNDERSTANDING WHAT THEATER MEANS.[03]

Die Einladung anzunehmen, einen Text über die Arbeit eines Künstlers zu schreiben, der sich selbst auf eine Vielzahl von Texten und unterschiedlichste Autoren bezieht, könnte dazu verführen, in diesen Arbeiten die Bausteine für ein Werk zu erkennen, die – nach dem Prinzip von Ursache und Wirkung – nur zusammengezählt werden müssten, um die finale Botschaft zu verstehen. In den Zitaten und Referenzen würden die von Cerith Wyn Evans namhaft gemachten Ursachen liegen, aus denen dieser seine Fragen und Extensionen ableiten würde, um dann seine Perspektiven auf die Realität und damit seine Arbeiten erklären zu können. Ohne vorgreifen zu wollen: Würde man versuchen, Theodor W. Adorno, John Cage, Jean-Luc Godard, William Burroughs, Guy Debord, Terry Wilson und Brion Gysin mit Madame de Lafayette, Eve Kosofsky Sedgwick, Pier Paolo Pasolini, Bertolt Brecht,

---

01 JEAN-LUC GODARD: *INTERVIEWS*, HRSG. VON DAVID STERRIT, MISSISSIPPI 1998. S. 41.

02 EBD., S. 14.

03 EBD.

Luigi Pirandello, Samuel Morse und Judith Butler zu einer Architektur des Arguments zusammenzutragen, dann wäre das Produkt dem Turmbau zu Babel nicht unähnlich: eine argumentative Baustelle für die Ewigkeit, und dennoch: ein Manifest des Irrationalen, das über das Rationale und den „Hausverstand" triumphiert.

Setzt man sich mit den verschiedenen Autoren und Referenzen in den Arbeiten von Cerith Wyn Evans auseinander, dann wird von diesen ob ihrer Differenz das Irrationale nicht als Beweis für die Grenzen des Rationalen apostrophiert, sondern der ideologische und politische Kern der irrationalen Rationalität freigelegt. Das Entziffern der mehrstimmigen Botschaften folgt weniger der Absicht, einen geheim gehaltenen Text zu verstehen, sondern die Wirkungen dieser irrationalen Rationalität, die man einfacher mit „common sense" übersetzen kann, zu beschreiben. In diesem Sinne handeln die Arbeiten von Cerith Wyn Evans von den Wirkungen einer gesellschaftlichen Übereinkunft, die das irrationale Machtverhältnis zwischen Menschen und Kulturen verdeckt, indem dieses erklärt und geklärt wird – als Auswirkung einer Ursache. Wenn die Referenzen und Texte, auf die sich Cerith Wyn Evans bezieht, trotz ihrer Heterogenität etwas gemeinsam haben, dann ist es dieser Zweifel an der Rationalisierung des Irrationalen, das verdeckt und verschleiert werden soll. Vor diesem Hintergrund gerät eine Analyse, die den Dingen auf den Grund gehen will, in die Krise, weil sie selbst Gefahr läuft, mit der Konstruktion eines Grundes eine Argumentation für die Realität bereit zu stellen, die angesichts ihrer politischen und sozialen Wirkungen in der Krise steckt. Anstelle die Wirkungen über die Konstruktion eines ursächlichen Grundes zu erklären, folgen die Arbeiten von Cerith Wyn Evans einer Analyse der Wirkungen.

Die Wirkungen vermitteln sich im Unterschied zu den Ursachen als wahrnehmbare Phänomene. Sie liegen nicht im Verborgenen, sondern an der Oberfläche. Wirkungen sind Erscheinungen, die ihren Grund verloren haben können oder nie einen Grund hatten. Weil es sich bei Wirkungen um wahrnehmbare Phänomene handelt, sind sie der

Gegenwart verhaftet – unabhängig davon, wie weit ihre Ursachen zurück liegen. Die Gegenwärtigkeit von Wirkungen zeitigt deshalb ein spezifisches Verhältnis zur Geschichte. Was historisch unterschiedlichen Epochen zugeordnet und zeitlich voneinander geschieden werden kann, tritt aus der Perspektive der Wirkungen in eine Phase der Gleichzeitigkeit – in ein simultanes „Noch". Wenn sich Cerith Wyn Evans auf einen Roman von Madame de Lafayette aus dem Jahr 1678 bezieht, dann deshalb, weil dieser Text trotz seiner historischen Dimension immer „noch" Fragen bereit stellt, die er mit jenen anderer Autoren und späteren Datums in Beziehung setzen kann. In ihrer Wirkung bilden sie trotz ihrer historischen Variablen eine virulente Gegenwart. Diese virulente Gegenwart erkennt in den Werken nicht nur den Inhalt, der erklärt und verstanden werden will, sondern eine performative Qualität, die darin besteht, dass diese immer noch und wieder in der Lage sind, auf die Wahrnehmung der Gegenwart einzuwirken – auch dann, wenn sie nicht verstanden werden können. Darin haben Wirkungen ihren irrationalen Gehalt, den man verstehen kann, ohne dessen Grund zu kennen.

In verschiedenen Interviews erzählt Cerith Wyn Evans von seinem ersten Aufenthalt in Tokio. Untergebracht hoch oben in einem Wolkenkratzer blickt Evans aus dem Fenster und sieht über das riesige Meer aus blinkenden Lichtern und … „I thought, if only I could tune in to what the city was saying, then there would be this vast, dense, polyphony of texts that are all somehow speaking at the same time, all over-riding each other, all reading at different speeds, that somehow …the city became this vast coded text. I was very interested in the notion of something being in code."[04]

Evans entschlüsselt die Stadt als Text, der entschlüsselt werden will, aber nicht entschlüsselt werden muss. Das Lichtermeer wirkt auf ihn wie ein Text, dessen Inhalt nicht verstanden und entziffert werden kann – und dennoch bleibt der Eindruck eines verschlüsselten Gehalts:

---

[04] CERITH WYN EVANS: *LOOK AT THAT PICTURE*…, KATALOG WHITE CUBE, LONDON 2003.

die performative Qualität eines Textes, der wirkt und spricht, ohne etwas sagen zu müssen. Was Cerith Wyn Evans mit diesem Eindruck beschreibt, ist eine Sprache, die nur in ihrer Sprachlichkeit erscheint, als reine Sprache, als Sprache in Potenz. Es ist nicht wichtig, was sie sagt, sondern dass sie etwas sagen kann – dass sie wirkt als Sprache, die einen Raum der Kommunikation bereit hält.

Wenn sich Cerith Wyn Evans auf Texte und Autoren bezieht und diese in seine Arbeiten integriert, dann stellt sich die Frage, ob seine Werke entschlüsselt werden wollen, indem man die Referenzen analysiert und versteht. Ginge es nur um dieses hermeneutische Unterfangen, dann bliebe aber eine andere Frage offen: Warum übersetzt Evans diese Texte etwa in eine Sprache, die auf dem Morse-Alphabet basiert, das selbst in die Jahre gekommen ist? Neue Informationstechnologien haben das Morsesystem abgelöst, das deshalb auch kaum mehr vom jemandem entziffert werden kann. Wenn man dem Künstler nicht unterstellen mag, dass er seine Zitate nur verschlüsselt, um seinen Arbeiten die Aura einer Geheimbotschaft zu verleihen, dann muss die Antwort anders ausfallen.

Das Morsealphabet, das von dem amerikanischen Maler und Erfinder Samuel Morse in den Anfängen der Moderne im frühen 19. Jahrhundert entwickelt wurde, basiert auf einem System aus kurzen oder langen Strichen, die mit Lichtsignalen oder Tönen, visuell wie akustisch, übertragen werden können. Dieses binäre System lässt die auf Leibniz zurückgehende Übersetzung der Zahlen in Folgen aus 0 und 1 genauso in Erinnerung rufen wie die moderne und impressionistische Analyse der Wahrnehmung, die die neurologische Botschaft vor die Bedeutung eines Bildes setzte: Bevor das Gehirn ein Bild erkennt, nimmt das Auge nur bedeutungslose Impulse wahr, die erst durch die Interpretation zu Farben, Formen und den entsprechenden Bedeutungen addiert werden. Analog dazu bleibt jemandem, dem die Zuordnung von kurzen und langen Strichfolgen zu Buchstaben nicht bekannt ist, der Inhalt der Botschaft verschlossen. Aber wenn auch die Botschaft nicht verstanden wird, so kann dennoch der Eindruck von Sprache wahrgenommen werden. Man kann an den Lichtsignalen erkennen, dass hier kommuniziert wird – dass es sich allein um eine unbekannte Sprache handelt, die gerade aufgrund ihrer Unverständlichkeit als reine Sprachlichkeit erscheint: nicht als Geheimnis, das entschlüsselt werden will, sondern als ein Bild der Sprache, als eine Sprache in Potenz. Die flackernden Lichter von Cerith Wyn Evans' Leuchter, die ins Morsealphabet übersetzte Texte wiedergeben, erzählen von einer Sprache, die unabhängig von ihrem Inhalt kommuniziert – wie das Lichtermeer über Tokio, das sich der Entschlüsselung entzieht und trotzdem Sprachlichkeit signalisiert.

Basierend auf dem Morsealphabet werden die Texte nicht primär als Inhalte übersetzt, sondern als Schrift: Buchstabe für Buchstabe, Strich für Strich, erscheinen die Texte im Licht der Leuchter wieder als Schrift. Das Begehren, die Texte auch lesen und verstehen zu können, wird über kleine Monitore erfüllt. Die Leuchter erfüllen eine andere Aufgabe. Wenngleich den Texten verpflichtet, sind sie der Schrift zugewandt: dem Schreiben als Prozess, der Bedeutung entstehen lässt – mit anderen Worten: der performativen Energie, die der Sprache innewohnt. Sprache wird nicht gefasst als Container, der etwas beinhaltet, sondern als Kraft, die in der Lage ist, etwas entstehen zu lassen, und sei es einen abstrakten Raum der Kommunikation. Schrift und Schreiben werden nicht begriffen als Technik, die einen Gedanken abbilden, sondern als Weg, der im Schreiben simultan einen Raum für Gedanken öffnet. Und was für das Schreiben gilt, gilt auch fürs Lesen: Buchstabe für Buchstabe entwickelt sich Bedeutung, die einen Inhalt als performative Figur entstehen lässt. Aus dieser Perspektive führt der Versuch, die verloren gegangene Schrift des Morsealphabets zu entziffern, wieder an eine Vorstellung des Lesens heran, die den Inhalt nicht zu trennen vermag von dem Abenteuer und Spektakel, das mit dem ersten Lesen, mit dem Verbinden von Buchstaben und Wörtern zu Bedeutungszusammenhängen, verbunden war: das Erlebnis von Sprache als ein Raum des Versprechens, als Botschaft, als Verheißung von Bedeutung.

Wenn hier von Schrift, Text und Sprache die Rede ist, dann in dem Sinne, der mit dem Morsealphabet entwickelt wurde: die Variabilität des Mediums, in dem sich Sprache artikulieren kann. Das System aus kurzen und langen Strichen ermöglicht – wie bereits erwähnt – die Übertragung der Zeichen in visuelle wie akustische oder elektrische Signale. Die Erscheinung von Sprache mag variieren: Ein Text mag übersetzt in Tonlängen wie ein Musikstück klingen – und übersetzt in Lichtsignale, die filmisch festgehalten werden, wie ein strukturalistischer Film aussehen. Erleuchten die Lichtimpulse gar einen Raum, wie die Leuchter von Cerith Wyn Evans, dann erscheint der Text in der Übersetzung als Mise en scène – als Sprachraum, der verspricht, was immer sich in diesem ereignet, im Licht einer Bedeutung, ja im Licht einer Erkenntnis wahrnehmen zu können.

Die Aufklärung, die im englischen „enlightenment" noch deutlicher die Verknüpfung von Erkenntnis und Lichtmetaphorik zum Ausdruck bringt, basierte auf der Vorstellung, das im Licht der Rationalität erscheinende Urteil festhalten und objektivieren zu können: wie die Fotografie den Augenblick. Verbunden mit dieser Ästhetik der Objektivierbarkeit war auch eine Vorstellung von Sprache, die in der Lage wäre, eine Erkenntnis abbilden und festhalten zu können: der Satz als Schnappschuss eines Gedankens, der sich im Licht der Rationalität nicht mehr als performative Figur versteht, sondern sich in den fixierbaren Grund und Ausgangspunkt für den nächsten Gedanken verwandelt, um in der Folge einen Raum des Wissens zu etablieren – als Wissen, das sich vermehren kann, ohne sich im Kern verändern zu müssen. Dieses Wissen im Zeitalter seiner wissenschaftlichen und methodischen Reproduzierbarkeit lebt von der Vorstellung, einen Gedanken unabhängig vom kulturhistorischen Kontext des Subjekts vermitteln zu können. Gilt der Gedanke für ein Subjekt, dann gilt er aufklärerisch auch für jedes andere. Dieses aufklärerische Subjekt ist angehalten, das Wissen als reproduzierbare Größe wahrzunehmen. Die Paradoxie dieses Unterfangens, dem aufgeklärten Subjekt zu huldigen und es zugleich in seiner Reproduzierbarkeit zu verlieren, charakterisierte den Widerspruch der Moderne im 19. Jahrhundert. War die Fotografie – eine fast gleichzeitige Erfindung wie das Alphabet von Morse – ein Medium, das vergleichbar dem rationalen Gedanken die Realität objektiv im Licht ihrer Erscheinung festhalten konnte, so war es der Film, der – trotz seiner Reproduzierbarkeit – der Gegenwart seiner Projektion und der unmittelbaren Wirkung auf das Subjekt verhaftet blieb. Wie das Subjekt beim Lesen Buchstabe für Buchstabe der Schrift folgen muss, so fordert der Film vom Subjekt eine Wahrnehmung, die dem Akt des Lesens verwandt ist: Wort für Wort, Bild für Bild, entwickeln sich Bedeutungen, die sich genauso wenig festhalten lassen wie die Vorstellung vom Subjekt. Markierte der Film schon im späten 19. Jahrhundert dieses Scheitern an einer Wahrnehmung, die das erkennende Subjekte zu fixieren suchte, so war es etwa Oscar Wilde, der in seinem zeitgleichen *Bildnis des Dorian Gray* eine analoge Geschichte erzählte. Das fixierbare Subjekt, das fixierbare Bild des Subjekts und die Vorstellung eines fixierbaren Wissens scheitern an einer Sprache, die eine Vorstellung der Realität fixieren möchte und dabei den performativen Akt des Sprechens, Lesens oder Wahrnehmens verkennt.

Der Film insistiert auf diese Aktivität der Wahrnehmung. Nur wer ihm folgt, kann ihm folgen: Im Unterschied zur Fotografie, die den Augenblick festhält, reißt der Film das Subjekt mit sich. Wenn man die Erkenntnis weiterhin mit einer Lichtmetaphorik assoziieren will, dann liefert der Film das Licht für die Erkenntnis in der Moderne. Dieses Licht ist keine konstante und metaphysische Kraft, die die Wahrheit ans Licht zerrt und aufklärend erhellt, sondern eine bewegliche und sich unentwegt verändernde Figur: reproduzierbar und dennoch im Wesen der Veränderung und dem Augenblick verschrieben – dem Schreiben mehr verbunden als dem Text. Im Angesicht des Films wird selbst der Text für den Film nur mehr im „Drehbuch" denkbar. Seine Beweglichkeit lässt das Buch rotieren. Auch im englischen „script" wird der Schrift und dem Akt des Schreibens die gleiche Bedeutung beigemessen wie dem finalen Text. So sehr ein Buch oder ein Text einen Inhalt fassen, so sehr wird dieser Inhalt aus der Perspektive der Moderne dem Augenblick des Lesens überantwortet. Was fix und reproduzierbar erscheint, gibt sich in der Wahrnehmung stets als veränderliche Dimension zu erkennen. Im Unterschied zur Aufklärung führt die Erkenntnis der Moderne nicht zu einem sich sukzessive konsolidierenden Subjekt, sondern dazu, dass sich das erkennende Subjekt durch die Erkenntnis selbst verändert. Mallarmés Öffnen des Textes in eine Schrift, die immer wieder und immer wieder anders gelesen und verstanden werden kann, erscheint im gleichzeitigen Licht der ersten Filmprojektoren nur allzu legitim.

Wenn Cerith Wyn Evans auf Leuchter aus der Moderne zurückgreift, um über diese seine ins Morsealphabet übersetzten „Schriften" in die Gegenwart einzuschreiben, immer wieder und je aufs Neue, dann erscheinen die zugrunde liegenden Texte in einer filmischen Perspektive. Obgleich sie aussehen wie Leuchter, ist das Licht, das sie spenden, dem flackernden Licht des Filmprojektors verwandt. Die Variabilität des Morsealphabet erlaubt Wyn Evans, die Texte wieder in „Drehbücher" und „scripts" zu übersetzen. Unabhängig von ihrer historischen Einbettung flackern sie in der Gegenwart ihrer Projektion, sie versprechen eine Sprachlichkeit, die den Inhalt nicht mehr zu trennen vermag von der Wahrnehmung durch ein Subjekt, das sich in der Wahrnehmung, ob im Schauen oder Lesen, stets mit verändert. Die in Drehbücher und Schriften übersetzten Texte verwandeln das Subjekt selbst im flackernden Licht in eine variierende Figur. „Erleuchtet" findet sich dieses Subjekt in einer Mise en scène wieder. So variabel das Morsealphabet übertragen werden kann, so variabel erscheint die übersetzte Schrift als Film, als Theater oder „script". Was man auf den ersten Blick wie eine Installation interpretieren kann, gibt sich beim zweiten Blick als Film, beim dritten als Theater und beim vierten als Leseraum zu erkennen. Die Frage, welche Rolle das Subjekt in dieser Inszenierung spielt, bleibt der jeweiligen Perspektive des Subjekts überantwortet. Ein Interesse an dieser Variabilität der Rolle hat Cerith Wyn Evans schon in einem anderen Interview signalisiert.

Darin erzählt er „begeistert" von einer Szene in Jean-Luc Godards *Zwei oder drei Dinge, die ich von ihr weiß* (1966): Godard filmt Marina Vlady, die als Schauspielerin Juliette Jeanson spielt, zwei Mal mit der gleichen Kameraeinstellung und in der gleichen Bewegung auf einem Balkon vor dem Hintergrund der Stadt. Die Offstimme erläutert beim ersten Shot: „Jetzt sehen wir die Schauspielerin Marina Vlady, sie stammt aus Russland, wir sehen sie von der linken Seite ..." und beim zweiten Shot erklärt die Offstimme: „Nun sehen wir Juliette Jeanson ...".[05] Die gleiche Person, der gleiche Ort, das gleiche Ereignis: und dennoch eine wesentliche Verschiebung innerhalb der Reproduktion, die das Subjekt in verschiedenen Rollen denkt.

Das Licht aus einer filmischen Perspektive mit einem Realitätsbegriff zu assoziieren, der in der Realität selbst eine projektive und variierende Figur erkennt, hat sich schon in anderen Arbeiten von Cerith Wyn Evans abgezeichnet. In *Has the film already started* (2000) hat Wyn Evans – wenn man so sagen will – einen Film wieder in Licht übersetzt. Er hat den Film *L´Anti-Concept* von Gil Wolman abgefilmt, indem er mit einer Kamera das Licht des Films direkt vor der Projektorlinse aufgenommen hat. Was bleibt, ist ein Film, der analog zum abgefilmten Film aus flackerndem Licht besteht, aber keine Motive mehr erkennen lässt – außer dem sich verändernden Licht als zentralem Motiv. Dieses Licht wird auf einen im Raum schwebenden Ballon projiziert, der dadurch trotz seiner Körperlichkeit und Dreidimensionalität die Funktion einer Projektionsfläche übernimmt. Was als *L´Anti-Concept*-Film konzipiert war, wird gegen das Konzept des Films wieder in einen filmischen Raum übersetzt, der nun aber wie die begehbare und sich im Licht verändernde Realität aussieht: eine theatralische Realität, eine Realität der Inszenierung, die der Frage, was der Film ist, dokumentarisch und realistisch verbunden bleibt. Jean-Luc Godard, der sich in dieser Frage wie Cerith Wyn Evans auf Brecht und Pirandellos *Sechs Personen suchen einen Autor* (*Six Character in Search of an Author*)

[05] VGL. HANS ULRICH OBRIST: *INTERVIEWS (CERITH WYN EVANS)*, VOL. 1, MAILAND 2003, S. 942F.

bezieht, soll hier antworten, „…to show the common ground between realism and theatricality. Each has its separate frontier but there are certain points at which they merge."[06]

In anderen Arbeiten wird diese Nahtstelle zwischen Film, Theater und Realität über eine „Leuchtschrift" markiert, die an der Wand montiert wird – als sei sie der Untertitel für einen verloren gegangenen Film, der nur mehr den filmischen Subtext für die Wahrnehmung der Realität hinterlassen hat: Der filmische Untertitel verwandelt die Realität in einen Film, dem hier allein die Bilder vorenthalten werden, um den Vorstellungsbildern angesichts der Realität Platz zu machen. Lautet ein Subtext „meanwhile…across town", der den Blick von Cerith Wyn Evans aus dem Tokioter Hotelfenster in Erinnerung rufen kann und die blinkende Stadt wie einen Monumentalfilm über endlose Textmengen erscheinen lässt, so markiert eine andere Leucht- und Lichtschrift in Form eines Möbiusbandes (1997) die ununterbrochene Verwandlung und Verkehrung von Innen und Außen, Schrift und Form, Bewegung und Wiederholung, Theater und Realität, Film und Theater, die in bestimmten Augenblicken ineinander übergehen.

Die Arbeit mit dem Medium Licht ermöglicht Cerith Wyn Evans die verschiedenen Medien und Genres miteinander zu verbinden. Wenn er auf der einen Seite Texte in Lichtsignale übersetzt, Filme wieder in „Lichtbilder" verwandelt und auf der anderen Seite die Schrift als Leuchtschrift räumlich inszeniert, dann entstehen mehrsprachige und mehrstimmige Räume, die sich auf den Film und auf das Theater genauso beziehen wie auf die Literatur und Theorie. Wenn in diesen Zeilen der Musik und dem Sound in den Arbeiten von Cerith Wyn Evans keine Aufmerksamkeit geschenkt wurde, so soll die Verknüpfung seiner verschiedenen Werke zu einem polyphonen Lichtkonzert doch erlaubt

---

[06] JEAN-LUC GODARD: *INTERVIEWS*. A.A.O., S. 5.

VGL. CERITH WYN EVANS, DER SEINE LEUCHTER IN EINEM INTERVIEW BESCHREIBT: „IT'S A MODERNIST, CLASSIC STEP BACK, A BRECHTIAN STEP BACK. IT'S THE SAME STEP THAT PIRANDELLO TOOK IN *SIX CHARACTERS IN SEARCH OF AN AUTHOR*." IN: CERITH WYN EVANS: *LOOK AT THAT PICTURE…*, A.A.O.

sein. Die Verwendung von Licht als integrativem Medium, das einem Autor erlaubt, Schriften, Texte und Filme zu einem räumlichen und theatralen Ereignis zu verbinden, wendet sich an eine Erkenntnismetapher, die sich der Augenblicklichkeit und Gegenwart verschrieben hat. Dieses Licht reißt alle Referenzen, die es in sich trägt, in eine konzertante Situation, die jeder Ausstellung den Charakter einer Aufführung verleiht. Dieser Aufführungscharakter ist es, der dem zitierten, übersetzten und impliziten Wissen, das in den verschiedenen Arbeiten zum Ausdruck kommt, eine Rolle zuschreibt, die einem zeitgenössischen Subjektbegriff angemessen erscheint. Bei diesem Wissen handelt es sich nicht um eine sukzessiv wachsende Architektur von Erkenntnissen, die nur mehr zusammengeführt werden müssten und einem in der Zukunft liegenden und unerreichbaren Ideal verbunden wären; dieses Wissen ist affektiver und temporärer Natur und wendet sich an sein Subjekt und dessen politische und diskursive Gegenwart – unfähig auf Distanz zu gehen, affiziert von den Wirkungen der heterogenen Erscheinungen von Realität und wissend um die eigene Rolle, die darin besteht, mehrere Rollen spielen zu müssen, ohne deren Ursachen verstehen zu können. Hat Foucault eine *Archäologie des Wissens* skizziert, so antwortet Wyn Evans mit einer Ästhetik des Wissens, die das alte Licht der Erleuchtung gegen das filmische Licht der Projektion getauscht hat. Dieses Wissen wirkt nicht durch einen *common sense*, in dem man sich auf eine gemeinsame Ursache und deren Wirkungen geeinigt hat, sondern in seiner Gegenwärtigkeit, die nur in der flackernden Aufmerksamkeit des Subjekts aufleuchtet. Wie die Arbeiten vom Licht leben, so lebt das Wissen von der Projektion des Erkennens.

JAN VERWOERT
AT NIGHT THEY TALK TO EACH OTHER ON THE RADIO

NOT A WORD ABOUT THE WORK
Is there another way to experience experiences, to speak language, and to know knowledge other than the one the world offers? In his art Cerith Wyn Evans conducts a speculative discourse on the conditions and potential to change the relationship of experience, speech, and knowledge. His installations are venues on which such a change could take place. Each work establishes a scenario that challenges us to find another possible outlook on the world. Cerith Wyn Evans creates these scenarios with gestures that are the acts of precisely thought-out arbitrariness: of a decision to put particular objects, texts, or images in relation to particular historical figures, events, and put discourses on a stage in a given place for a particular time to see how they react to one another when an audience is introduced. Instead of scenarios, one might also call them "ceremonies": the feeling that comes with getting involved in a work by Cerith Wyn Evans is comparable to the feeling of participating in a ceremony whose protocol is defined by the elements and frame conditions of the given work, although its outcome remains open. In terms of its ceremonial character, the structure of his works corresponds in many respects to the structure of a séance. The sequence of a séance is regulated by protocols: formalized techniques are employed and particular spirits are called upon. However, whether these spirits, or perhaps others in their place, will appear, and what they have to say, cannot be predicted.

Cerith Wyn Evans's work thus shows what a praxis of speculative thought is concerned with. Speculative thought does not impose particular results. It merely allows results. It merely sees to it that something results, that something happens, that something is decided. Speculative thought gives itself over to its own dynamic and allows itself to be driven, by its own interests, desires, and whims, to places where decisions result. What decision is made is of secondary importance. In fact, the decision really only counts as an event that attracts new events and does not end the process of speculation but rather extends it. Speculative thought is thus motivated here by its own contradictions. It does not resolve them but generates them in order to observe them from all sides. It enthusiastically formulates paradoxes in constantly new variations or observes variations of the same paradox in various formulations.

The speculative trait in Cerith Wyn Evans's work is thus clearly seen in the way it mobilizes contradictions. One such contradiction is that between arbitrariness and precision. It is never entirely clear in this work whether the compilation of its elements is based on a meticulously choreographed composition or on pure improvisation. Are thought-out connections being produced here or are fundamentally different things being thrown together according to the whim of a moment? One guiding principle of speculative thought is that it doesn't care about its own justification. It is constantly crossing the line over to thoughtlessness. In this manner of thinking, knowledge is something that is available and that has to be squandered. Speculative thought recognizes the thoughtless approach to knowledge as the only acceptable one, because it is the only one that does not manage knowledge as property or accumulate it as capital but instead exists only by means of its constant investment. The satisfying thing about the work of Cerith Wyn Evans is that he squanders knowledge. He eradicates knowledge as capital by investing in the process of a way of thinking that is not compelled to yield a profit. The ethics of speculative thought that shapes Cerith Wyn Evans's work thus lies more in an irresponsibility with regard to the rationales for this way of thought that is based on a feeling of responsibility to the liberation of thought. This attitude is based on the insight that new meaning can be produced only when one takes the risk of producing complete nonsense, because the distinction between sense and nonsense can only ever be made ex post facto, after thought has ceased, and not even then with certainty. It would be arrogant to believe one could decide in advance to think sensibly. Keeping the distinction between sense and nonsense open, by contrast, demonstrates respect for the future.

We are never the ones who decide what is sense and what nonsense; it is always others in the future who do. Speculative thought respects this by remaining open. This makes it inviting. The reason Cerith Wyn Evans's work feels inviting, why one always feels welcome as a visitor in his installations, is that he allows us to decide about the meaning of his work. The value of the knowledge and the meaning of the thinking that he presents are still indeterminate at the moment when we respond to the work. But only when the value of the meaning and knowledge are not taken for granted do we understand it. The principle of speculative thought is to induce a state of indeterminacy that reveals the possible value of a decision precisely by showing that it has not yet been made. Speculative thought presents the contrasting options for a decision that a contradiction offers us as pure potentialities.

This principle of speculative thought determines at the same time a change in our attitude toward experience, toward the thinking and knowledge that the works of Cerith Wyn Evans provoke. The attitude in question is the radical openness that is the goal of speculative thought. The paradoxical aspect of this openness is that it creates obligations with regard to aesthetics, ethics, and epistemology. The importance of a decision can only be determined if the decision is not made for us. The urgency of thinking can only be grasped if its own task is not declared already finished. The whole approach of Cerith Wyn Evans's work is committed to an ethics that rejects the capital-ridden management of knowledge as property. One way to respond to this obligation would be not to waste words over it and not to accumulate knowledge about it, in order to avoid creating the false impression that this sort of thing would be necessary, and instead to write about the work's principle – the speculative – in a tone that conforms to that principle. This is an attempt to do so.

FROM EXPERIENCE
Attempting to portray Cerith Wyn Evans's work as a purely speculative

discourse may, in principle, be justified. Such a portrayal is, however, problematic, since it lies at a maximum of abstraction from the moment of experience in which precisely those qualities of the work are manifested that the language of argumentation can only invoke. When one speaks of experiences, one must describe them also.

I can still recall quite precisely the moment when I first saw *Cleave 03 (Transmission, Vision of the Sleeping Poet)*, at the 50th Venice Biennale of Art in 2003. I was aware of the work's conception from conversations leading up to the exhibition,[01] and thus I knew that the work would have a searchlight of the kind used by American troops for air defense in the Second World War. It would be installed on Giudecca Island, off Venice, as part of an exhibition of Welsh artists in the garden of a palazzo. It was to send light signals in Morse code straight up into the sky. (In this context I was also aware that Morse code has lost its meaning as a universal means of communication and is scarcely used anymore today, so that this code is really a language from the past.) I had been informed that the text being broadcast into the sky by Morse code, which had been encoded automatically by a computer program, was from *Gweledigaethau y Bardd Cwsc* (Visions of the sleeping bard) of 1703, by the Welsh author Ellis Wynne. It is a classic work of Welsh literature that describes the ecstatic experience of a writer who is borne by angels into the sky and looks down on the world from the air (only to see Venice as the greatest den of iniquity on the planet). It had also been explained to me that the idea and plot of Wynne's book were based on *Sueños y discursos* (*Dreams and discourses*) of 1627, by the Spanish author Francisco de Quevedo, whose text would be transmitted in Morse code by a simple lamp in the exhibition *Utopia Station* in the Arsenale in Venice. On the conceptual level, therefore, I had a clear idea of the messages contained in the Morse code of these two ghostly dialogues with

---

[01] "CERITH WYN EVANS IN CONVERSATION WITH JAN VERWOERT," IN *FURTHER: ARTISTS FROM WALES AT THE FIFTIETH INTERNATIONAL ART EXHIBITION, VENICE* (CARDIFF: WALES ARTS INTERNATIONAL, 2003), 70–85.

each other: an avowal of the utopian power of ecstatic experiences to transcend the existing order of the world and to open up a space in which texts whose voices are no longer bound to concrete subjects are related to each other in a communication that bridges space and time and gives shape to an autonomous sphere of the imagination in which two texts communicate with each other without human intervention.

I had heard that a test run of the apparatus had been planned for the evening before the opening of the Biennale, but I had forgotten that immediately, and at night I was walking on the street, talking to friends, and had happened to look up to see a beam of light shooting straight up into the night sky, far above all the rooftops of the city. And just at that moment it faded briefly, only to light up again, as if it wanted to let me know by this winking that it saw that I saw it. At that moment I realized that all my prior knowledge had not in any way prepared me for the experience of seeing the work realized. The conceptual horizon of the work was for that moment merged with the feeling "There it is now." And this feeling was totally euphoric in a surprising way. This euphoria resembles the triumphant feeling that can overcome one when seeing amazing architectonic structures that seem to defy gravity and that thus communicate a feeling of a freedom that refuses to be bound by any laws, much less those of nature, the feeling "And it works!"

An essential aspect of the intensity of this experience was the feeling that the light signal had made me a witness to a sublime impertinence. My first thought was: what gives someone the right to produce something so beautiful? A form sublime in its simplicity, but one that was not content with its simplicity and began to communicate with me, and to do so in a surprisingly intimate way. The Morse code became innuendo. The monumental beam of light seemed to be blinking at me. (Like a diva who gazes down from the stage at one person in the audience.) This blinking at me makes me a confidante in an act, of the staging of a sublime spectacle that is justified only by its own arbitrariness, and hence of the shameless assertion: "Here, this is pretty. You know that and want that too, right?"

The unexpected intimacy of the feeling of being spoken to by a beam of light was, however, immediately accompanied by the knowledge that I was not the only one seeing the signal, that in fact this signal could be seen from far away, and so potentially everyone in Venice or the vicinity who looked up into the night sky could feel they were being addressed by the blinking beam of light. Most likely, however, no one else would be in a position to decode this signal, unless there happened to be someone in Venice who knew both Morse code and Welsh. That idea began a new chain of associations: who would be the ideal recipient of the signal if not a figure from a nineteenth-century novel (a Welshman traveling the world by sea, for example, who, for some reason that required a long story to explain, happened to be in Venice at the time)? Thus the number of potential addressees of this work is increased. With whom was the beam of light communicating? With me? With everyone? With itself? Or with another transmitter: a lamp in the Arsenale that is sending the Morse code of a second text? The fact that an essential aspect of *Cleave 03* – the question of the work's potential addressee – is left undecided in a crucial way reveals the speculative character of the work. The addressee is turned from a reality into a potential.

The same is true of the work's conception. The face of the finished work changes the status of the conception fundamentally. Before one experiences the realization, the conception is a piece of knowledge that one could take to be an explanation, justification, or rationale for the work. At the moment it is experienced, however, it becomes clear that the work is not explained, justified, or rationalized by its concept. Its only legitimation is its existence, the brute fact of the finished gesture. The fact that the beam of light is staggeringly beautiful is justification enough. Depriving the conception of the status of a justification is, however, not to say that the conception is obsolete. On the contrary, it becomes even more valuable, because it is released from a clear function and liberated. Faced with the brute fact of the realized work, the conception of the work is transformed into a horizon of possible questions that could be asked in relation to the work: How might the histories of the texts by and the figures of Wynne and de Quevedo themselves relate to each other and to the cultural phenomenon of Morse code? Who is speaking here with whom? In what language? About what? And above all: what language, what knowledge, and what dimension of experience is constituted by a communication that is directed simultaneously at me, at everyone, and at no one? To whom does a language speak that speaks itself, that speaks with itself, because no one else speaks it anymore, even though its effect as a signal speaks to everyone?

The crucial speculative feature of the work is thus revealed in the way it transforms the status of the knowledge on which it is based. One might say: *Cleave 03* twists the position of knowledge in time in relation to the time at which the work is realized. The speculation turns time on its axis: whereas the knowledge *prior* to the experience of the realized work could be conceived as something that *precedes* the work in the form of a conception, justification, or rationale, the knowledge can now be experienced as something that could only be produced by the work, as something that *procedes* from the work and is projected into the future in the form of a question, as *potential* not *real* knowledge: what the work knows, no one knows yet. It is a knowledge that can only be produced by answering the questions in the future, that throws open the work. And even this is not absolutely certain, since, in the end, it cannot be ruled out that the vanishing lines that the work sketches for a future way of thinking might not be false paths.

MODEL: THE POTENTIALITIES OF FIELDS

It is therefore characteristic of *Cleave 03* that it is a projection (in the truest sense of the work) of thoughts that have yet to be thought. Potentialities are the object of experience. That is why the experience of potentiality, even when it could be content with its own beauty, pushes beyond itself toward an abstraction of itself. Experience is anchored materially in reality (for technical reasons, the projection could be seen on site for only one week). Nevertheless, it possesses the status of a model. It asserts itself as a model of another language, a future knowledge, and an experience that is at once concrete and abstract. For that reason, it seems justified to abstract it from experience again and attribute the character of a model to it. That thinking in models is a fundamental feature of speculative thought is clear from a reading of Gilles Deleuze. In it we find a style of thinking that, audaciously and with relish, borrows metaphors from other discourses and builds valid philosophical models with them. Deleuze's models clarify the importance of speculative thought in two ways: First, they are attempts to describe what constitutes speculative thought. Second, however, they are the most intrinsic form of expression of this speculative thought, which progresses by sketching imaginative models of what it could be.

One model that could be interesting in related to the work of Cerith Wyn Evans is the metaphor of potentialities that Deleuze borrowed from mathematics and physics. In differential calculus the term "power" (if I understand it correctly) refers to differential quotients. Deleuze explains: "Power is the form of reciprocal determination according to which variable magnitudes are taken to be functions of one another."[02] In functional calculus, the relationship of the variable magnitudes of a differential – of a power – can be used to describe the path of a curve and hence a movement that is, as Deleuze interprets it, nevertheless unique at each of its points. Deleuze is not concerned here with identifying a principle that describes the continuity of a movement that produces new singularities at every stage of its virtual progression. This principle is a specific difference, a defined relationship between two variable magnitudes that as a potentiality becomes the

---

[02] GILLES DELEUZE, *DIFFERENCE AND REPETITION*, TRANS. PAUL PATTON (LONDON: ATHLONE, 1994),174.

driving force of a movement. In physics, in turn, the energy that derives entirely from the specific relationship of two objects to each other is called "potential energy" (the energy that an object obtains when its position is changed relative to other objects, as, for example, when it is raised and thus put in a position to do "work" by falling). It is only through the determination of a mutual relationship within a field of objects that potential energy is built up in the field. Deleuze calls this energy "intensity."[03]

The construction of this model has (at least) two points to make about a determination of what constitutes speculative thought. First, the potential of speculative thought lies in its ability to relate things and terms in unexpected ways and thus set them in motion, putting them in a position to do work and produce something singular. Second, the energy that thinking produces is not an energy that is exerted by a subject. It is rather the relationships themselves that construct the thinking which produces this energy. The thinking produces a field from whose differential structure all subsequent developments follow of their own accord. The field is the subject of the potentialities. Interestingly, today's parapsychology operates with a similar model taken from quantum physics. It has been observed that elements in closed systems can enter into relationships with one another, generate energy, and trigger processes without coming into direct physical contact. These are called "nonlocal correlations." If in the course of a séance, for example, objects begin to move or a medium perceives things that are taking place at another location, these are declared to be "nonlocal correlations." Within a certain field various processes harmonize in such a way that their structural communication produces current results.[04]

In principle, Cerith Wyn Evans's current installations can be described

---

[03] IBID., 236.

[04] ON THIS, SEE WALTER VON LUCADOU IN HIS PREFACE TO IDEM, *DIMENSION PSI: FAKTEN ZUR PARAPSYCHOLOGIE* (N.P.: LIST, 2003).

using this model of fields of potentialities. Their true artistic gesture consists in producing a field by placing various things in relationships to one another, with the goal that this field then builds up potentialities from its own dynamic, produces intensities, and sets unexpected processes in motion. The point is to produce a field that works. It is no coincidence, therefore, that the subject-less dynamic that the field sets in motion as a result of its potentialities resembles the ghostly character of processes that could happen as part of a séance. (Nor is it a coincidence that in 1847, shortly after Samuel Morse sent his first telegram in Morse code in 1844, the daughters of the Fox family, Methodists in Hydesville, New York, heard the rapping of ghosts from the walls of their house and replied to it, thus founding the modern spiritualist movement.[05] The history of modern communications media is thus connected with the beginnings of reports on ghostly occurrences and unforeseen interferences.)

The installation *Look at This Picture...How Does It Appear to You Now? Does It Seem to Be Persisting?* (2003) is just such a field that performs work. It establishes a relationship between a series of objects, discourses, and people. Five different texts are continuously translated into Morse code by computers. The coded signals are then broadcast by means of five different chandeliers whose bulbs light up and fade according to the frequency of the signal. The chandeliers create a splendid effect. Most are made of glass, but they differ greatly in form. This creates the impression that each chandelier lends an individually distinct sensory appearance, a particular theatrical presence, to the text that it transmits. Five flat-screen displays on the end wall of the installation space enable us to follow the process automated encoding. The text passage being sent at any given time appears here in parallel to the graphic notation of the Morse code.

A chandelier with twelve sweeping arms, produced by Barovier&Toso,

---

[05] ON THIS, SEE MICHAEL KRAJEWSKI, "MEDIUMISTISCHE WESEN ALS KÜNSTLER," *KUNSTFORUM INTERNATIONAL*, VOL. 163 (JANUARY–FEBRUARY 2003), 56.

transmits Terry Wilson's 1982 interview with Brion Gysin, "Goodnight Eileen," in which Gysin recounted his memories of the medium Eileen Garrett, whose prediction of a military accident led first to her arrest and then to work for the CIA. A lamp with a functionalist design of spherically arranged lightbulbs, manufactured by Achille Castiglione, transmits the novel *La princesse de Clèves* (1678), a story of romantic love that is organized into multiple perspectives and was probably written by various members of Madame de Lafayette's salon. A large, round chandelier made up of thin glass rods, produced by Venini Quadratti, transmits John Cage's associative aphorisms from his *Diary: How to Improve the World (You Will Only Make Matters Worse), Continued 1968 (Revised)*. A chandelier of glass calyxes, produced by Galliano Ferro, transmits the essay "Paranoid Reading and Reparative Reading; or, You're So Paranoid, You Probably Think This Essay Is about You" (2003), Eve Kosofsky Sedgwick's theoretical reflections on the imaginary position of the reader in a text while reading. A festive chandelier called the Lustre Marie-Thérèse, presumably designed for the Palais des Beaux Arts in Brussels, transmits the essay "The Stars Down to Earth" (1957) by Theodor W. Adorno, which is a critical analysis of modern spiritualism as a conformist approval of a feeling of being controlled by others and the reification of thinking.

The necessity for such a thorough description makes it clear just how precisely the details of the elements in the installation are defined. The tension that the work builds up as a field, however, lies precisely in the fact that these in themselves clearly determined elements are placed in a relation to one another that is left indeterminate in a crucial way. Naturally it is possible, in principle, to become oriented within the field that this installation opens up, if we understand it as a discourse and assign the chandeliers and their signals to the various texts and authors, identifying the latter in turn with particular traditions of thought. Following that line, one could say that the work presents a confrontation between the school of analytical, critical thinking and a school of speculative thinking that ecstatically transcends limits.

About the specific effects that the discourse collected here produce as an ensemble, however, it says as little as it does about the relationship that I establish with these works when I view this work. How do the components react with one another? On what level do they communicate with one another and with me? On the level of a discourse on content or on the level of a purely aesthetic experience? Although all the elements of the scene can be determined, it remains an open question what kind of a scenario it is. In this openness there is a potential for tension that turns the installation into a field.

The work that creates this field can be provisionally described as a processing of knowledge that puts me as a viewer into a different relationship with that knowledge. The field's work has its own dynamic, which frees me of the obligation to know. The computers are already processing the knowledge. They are doing the work of visualizing knowledge automatically. The discourse is completely automated. The didactic insistence that art be exploited as education, through an appropriate and internalization of its knowledge, is annulled. The automatons fulfill the obligatory program. I am left with the pleasure of being able to approach the mediated knowledge with a luxuriously irresponsible "interpassive" attitude. When the discourse is communicated as a stream of signals flowing without a subject, transmitted by the extravagantly beautiful chandeliers, what is left for me to do but give in to this stream? The appropriate reaction to the process that the work as a field sets in motion is to get into the atmosphere that it produces and let yourself go. Tune in and drop out. That is the protocol that I must follow to exploit the potentiality of the work through experience. This experience resembles that of a séance: the mysteriousness of the light signals and the auratic materiality of the chandeliers conveys a feeling of the ghostly presence of the assembled authors, both living and dead, in one room.

Once the significance of knowledge has been annulled by its automation, its significance is reconstituted in an unforeseen way on a new plane. The significance of the discourse is manifested in the signals of the chandeliers as shapeless and yet personified thought. For example, if I follow the signals of Adorno's chandelier, I can't help but get the impression that someone is speaking to me. Adorno's spirit materializes before my eyes in the lighting, and especially the dimming, of the lights, which never go out completely before they light up again. Inevitably, therefore, they recall the breathing of a human being, which also never comes to a stop, but merely marks the beginning of a new breathing motion. This experience has nothing to do with being moved by faith. After all, the message of this spirit is a virtuoso, mocking rejection of the delusion of spiritualism. The author's phantom compels me to follow the spirit of the text which is the spirit of critique; in other words, the atmosphere of the work allows me to experience critique as *potential*.

The experience of a ghostly present of texts and their authors communicated by the light signals of auratic chandeliers is the experience of intellectual potentialities. This experience of potentiality is not self-contained. It does not have the certainty of an experience in the here and now. The crucial aspect of this experience (which is what makes it resemble the experience of a séance) is of course precisely the dissolution of the unity of space and time: the assembled discourses and authors derive from different times and cultural spaces. These differences do not annul their assembly here. Their temporal relation to one another is synchronicity of the asynchronous; its spatial relation is "nonlocal correlation." The historical coordinates of the time frame in which the spirits of these texts and authors meet are as indeterminate as the spatial coordinates of their proximity and distance. Have these authors ever come in contact with one another? Do they refer to one another in their texts? Is their connection already a historical fact? Or are they meeting here and now for the first time? Has the intellectual potentiality in their encounter already discharged or is it just building up? Are these authors close to one another or does their thought remain foreign to the others? It remains impossible to determine the relationship among the spirits convened here. It is only certain that this relationship is intense: they are constantly sending one another signals. You can see that. On the one hand, their connection should be thought of speculatively as pure possibility. On the other, however, their connection is also experienced in the installation as a reality that can be perceived by the senses.

This paradox reveals the core of the experience of potentiality that produces the exhibition: it is the experience of real virtualities. The connection among the ghosts of the authors in the room is real and virtual at the same time. The discourse between them is historically possible; it is a potentiality of the history of thought. This historical potentiality is, however, not a historical fact. After all, the work is only producing it now, in the present. The historical significance of this potentiality can thus be measured only within the framework of its potential reception, and that means in the future. Just like *Cleave 03, Look at This Picture...How Does It Appear to You Now? Does It Seem to Be Persisting?* displaces in time the site of its significance, from the history of ratified knowledge to the future of speculative thought. By making it possible to experience as real virtuality the potentiality of thinking and the potentiality of a connection between different forms of thought, Cerith Wyn Evans complies with the central concern of speculative thought: conceiving the relationship between the possible and the real not as a difference but as a paradoxical synchronicity. To say of his works that they stage real virtualities means: here everything is like what it would be if it were like it is. But this says almost nothing about the utopian potential that is inherent in this view.

TRANSLATED FROM THE GERMAN BY STEVEN LINDBERG.

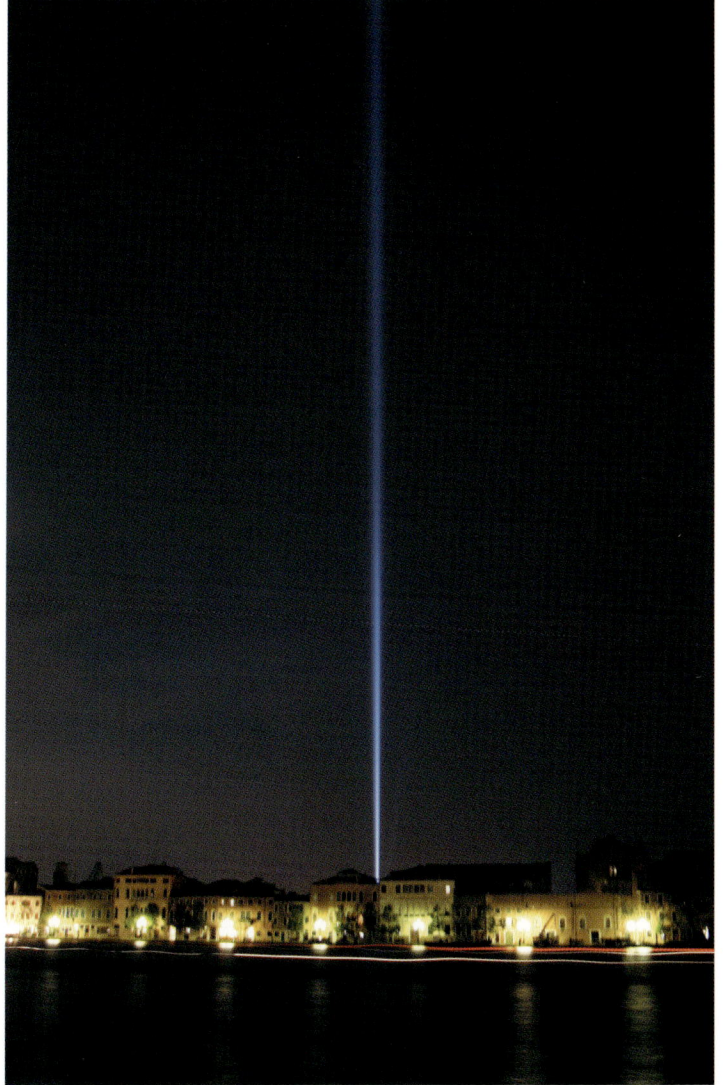

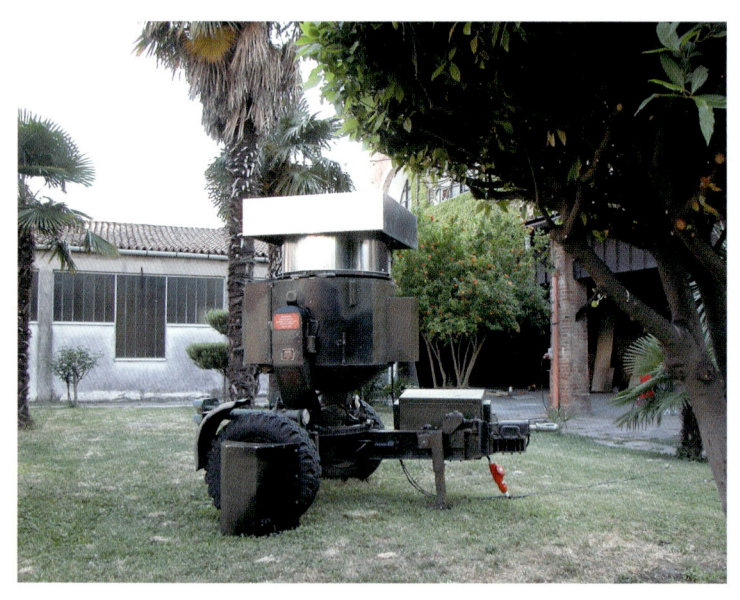

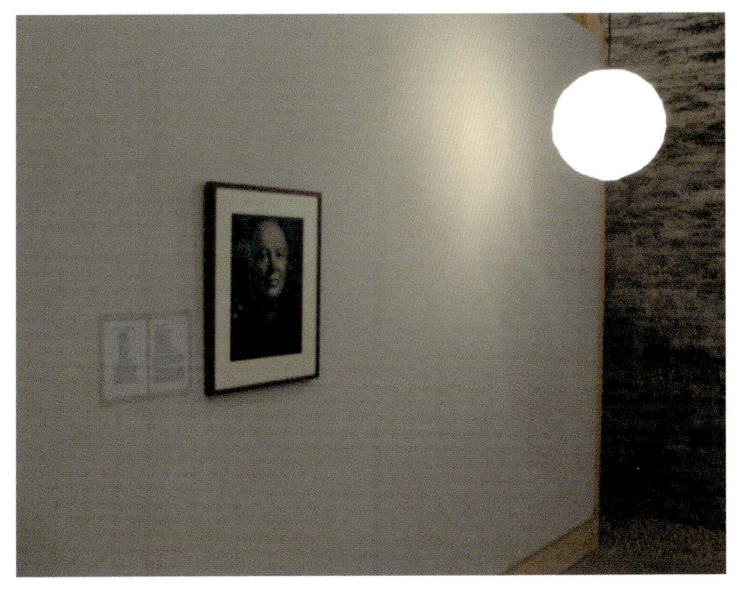

Cleave 03 (Transmission: Visions of the Sleeping Poet), 2003
World War II search light, shutter, computer, Morse code controlling device, text by Ellis Wynne
Dimensions variable

Flute, begin with me, 2003
Clear incandescent light bulb, Noguchi lampshade, light fitting, cable, imitation Morse code simulation unit, wall text in Welsh, framed photograph
Dimensions variable

JAN VERWOERT
NACHTS SPRECHEN SIE MITEINANDER IM RADIO

KEIN WORT ÜBER DIE ARBEIT
Gibt es eine andere Art und Weise, Erfahrungen zu erfahren, Sprache zu sprechen und Wissen zu wissen, als jene, die die Welt vorgibt? In seiner Kunst führt Cerith Wyn Evans einen spekulativen Diskurs über die Bedingungen und Potenziale der Veränderung des Verhältnisses zur Erfahrung, zur Sprache und zum Wissen. Seine installativen Arbeiten sind Schauplätze, an denen eine solche Veränderung stattfinden könnte. Jede Arbeit schafft ein Szenarium, das ein andere mögliche Einstellung zur Welt herausfordert. Diese Szenarien entwirft Cerith Wyn Evans mit Gesten, die Akte präzise durchdachter Willkür sind: der Entscheidung, bestimmte Objekte, Texte oder Bilder mit Bezug zu bestimmten historischen Personen, Ereignissen und Diskursen an einem Ort für eine Zeit zusammen auf die Bühne zu bringen und zu sehen, wie sie miteinander unter Einbeziehung eines Publikums reagieren. Statt von Szenarien könnte man auch von Zeremonien sprechen: Das Gefühl, sich auf eine Arbeit von Cerith Wyn Evans einzulassen, gleicht dem Gefühl, an einer Zeremonie teilzunehmen, deren Protokoll durch die Elemente und Rahmenbedingungen der Arbeit definiert ist, deren Ausgang aber offen bleibt. Von ihrem zeremoniellen Charakter her entspricht der Aufbau seiner Arbeiten in vielerlei Hinsicht der Struktur einer Séance: Der Ablauf einer Séance ist durch Protokolle geregelt, formalisierte Techniken werden zur Anwendung gebracht, bestimmte Geister werden angerufen – nur ob diese Geister oder vielleicht andere an ihrer Stelle erscheinen und was sie mitzuteilen haben, lässt sich im Vorhinein nicht sagen.

Die Arbeit von Cerith Wyn Evans zeigt so, worum es in einer Praxis spekulativen Denkens geht. Spekulatives Denken drängt nicht auf bestimmte Ergebnisse. Es lässt Ergebnisse zu. Es legt es darauf an, dass sich etwas ergibt, dass etwas passiert, dass etwas entschieden wird. Das spekulative Denken überlässt sich seiner eigenen Dynamik und lässt sich von seinen eigenen Interessen, Lüsten und Launen zu Punkten treiben, an denen sich Entscheidungen ergeben. Wie die Entscheidung ausfällt, ist zweitrangig. Eigentlich zählt die Entscheidung nur als ein Ereignis, das neue Ereignisse nach sich zieht und den Prozess der Spekulation nicht beendet, sondern verlängert. Das spekulative Denken motiviert sich dabei durch seine eigenen Widersprüche. Es löst sie nicht auf, sondern produziert sie, um sie von allen Seiten zu betrachten. Es begeistert sich dafür, Paradoxa in immer neuen Variationen zu formulieren, beziehungsweise in verschiedenen Formulierungen Variationen desselben Paradoxons zu erblicken.

Der spekulative Zug der Arbeit von Cerith Wyn Evans zeigt sich in diesem Sinne deutlich in der Art und Weise, wie sie Widersprüche mobilisiert. Ein solcher Widerspruch ist der zwischen Willkür und Präzision. In Bezug auf die Arbeit ist nie ganz zu klären, ob die Zusammenstellung ihrer Elemente auf einer minutiös durchchoreografierten Komposition oder auf reiner Improvisation beruht. Werden hier durchdachte Verbindungen hergestellt oder aus einer momentanen Lust heraus grundverschiedene Dinge zusammengeworfen? Ein Leitprinzip spekulativen Denkens ist, dass es sich nicht um seine Rechtfertigung schert. Es bewegt sich ständig auf der Grenze zur Gedankenlosigkeit. Wissen kommt in diesem Denken als etwas vor, das vorhanden ist und verschwendet werden muss. Das spekulative Denken erkennt im gedankenlosen Umgang mit Wissen die einzig akzeptable Umgangsform, weil auf diese Weise das Wissen nicht als Besitz verwaltet oder als Kapital akkumuliert wird, sondern nur in seiner fortwährenden Investition existiert. Das Befreiende an der Arbeit von Cerith Wyn Evans ist, dass er Wissen verschleudert. Er vernichtet Wissen als Kapital, indem er es in den Prozess eines Denkens investiert, das nicht unter dem Zwang steht, einen Ertrag abwerfen zu müssen. Die Ethik des spekulativen Denkens, die die Arbeit von Cerith Wyn Evans formuliert, liegt daher in einer aus dem Gefühl der Verantwortlichkeit gegenüber der Freisetzung des Denkens heraus begründeten Unverantwortlichkeit im Umgang mit den Rechtfertigungen dieses Denkens.

Diese Haltung beruht auf der Einsicht, dass sich neuer Sinn nur dann herstellen lässt, wenn man das Risiko eingeht, völligen Unsinn zu produzieren, aus dem Grunde, weil die Unterscheidung zwischen Sinn und Unsinn immer nur ex post facto, nach Ende des Denkens und dann auch noch nicht einmal mit Sicherheit zu treffen ist. Es wäre arrogant, zu glauben, man könne sich im Voraus darauf festlegen, sinnvoll zu denken. Die Unterscheidung zwischen Sinn und Unsinn offen zu halten, zeugt hingegen von Respekt gegenüber der Zukunft. Was Sinn ist und was Unsinn, entscheidet man nie selbst, sondern immer erst die anderen in der Zukunft. Spekulatives Denken respektiert dies durch seine Offenheit. Das macht es einladend. Der Grund, warum die Kunst von Cerith Wyn Evans einladend wirkt, warum man sich als BetrachterIn in seinen Installationen willkommen fühlt, ist, dass er einem die Entscheidung über den Sinn seiner Arbeit überlässt. Der Wert des Wissens und der Sinn des Denkens, das er inszeniert, sind in dem Moment, in dem man die Arbeit rezipiert, noch unentschieden. Aber erst wenn er nicht vorausgesetzt ist, begreift man den Wert von Sinn und Wissen. Das Prinzip spekulativen Denkens ist es, eine Unentschiedenheit herbeizuführen, die den möglichen Wert einer Unterscheidung gerade dadurch erkennen lässt, dass sie noch nicht getroffen ist. Spekulatives Denken stellt die entgegengesetzten Entscheidungsoptionen, die ein Widerspruch anbietet, als reine Potenziale aus.

Dieses Prinzip des spekulativen Denkens bestimmt zugleich die Veränderung der Einstellung zur Erfahrung, zum Denken und Wissen, die die Arbeiten von Cerith Wyn Evans provozieren. Die Haltung, um die es geht, ist die radikale Offenheit, auf die das spekulative Denken abzielt. Das Paradoxe an dieser Offenheit ist, dass sie in ästhetischer, ethischer und epistemologischer Hinsicht Verbindlichkeiten schafft. Das Gewicht der Entscheidung lässt sich erst dann ermessen, wenn sie einem nicht abgenommen wird. Die Dringlichkeit des Denkens lässt sich erst begreifen, wenn es seine eigene Aufgabe noch nicht für erledigt erklärt. Durch ihre ganze Art verpflichtet die Arbeit von Cerith Wyn Evans zu einer Ethik der Verweigerung der kapitalträchtigen Verwaltung von Wissen als Besitz. Eine Art, auf diese Verpflichtung einzugehen, wäre also, kein Wort über sie zu verlieren und kein

Wissen über sie zu akkumulieren, um den falschen Eindruck zu vermeiden, so etwas sei nötig, und anstelle dessen in einem Tonfall, der dem Prinzip der Arbeit entspricht, über ihr Prinzip, das Spekulative, zu schreiben. Dies sei hiermit versucht.

AUS DER ERFAHRUNG

Der Versuch, die Arbeit von Cerith Wyn Evans als rein spekulativen Diskurs darzustellen, mag prinzipiell berechtigt sein. Problematisch ist diese Darstellung dennoch, denn sie abstrahiert maximal von dem Moment der Erfahrung, in dem sich genau jene Qualitäten der Arbeit manifestieren, die eine argumentative Sprache nur beschwören kann. Wenn man von Erfahrungen spricht, muss man sie auch beschreiben. Also:

Ich kann mich noch sehr genau an den Moment erinnern, an dem ich *Cleave 03 (Transmission, Vision of the Sleeping Poet)* auf der 50. Venedig Biennale 2003 zum ersten Mal gesehen habe. Ich kannte die Konzeption der Arbeit aus Gesprächen im Vorfeld[01] und wusste daher, dass es sich bei der Arbeit um einen im zweiten Weltkrieg von amerikanischen Truppen zur Flugabwehr eingesetzten Suchscheinwerfer handeln würde, der, auf der Venedig vorgelagerten Insel Guidecca im Garten eines Palazzo in einer Ausstellung walisischer KünstlerInnen installiert, Leuchtsignale im Morsecode senkrecht in den Himmel sendet. (Mir war in diesem Zusammenhang auch bekannt, dass der Morsecode seine Bedeutung als universales Kommunikationsmittel verloren hat und heute kaum noch verwendet wird, dass es sich bei diesem Code also um die Sprache einer vergangenen Zeit handelt.) Ich war darüber informiert, dass es sich bei dem Text, der, durch ein Computerprogramm automatisch codiert, auf diese Weise in den Himmel gemorst werden würde, um den Text des Buches *Gweledigaethau y Bardd Cwsc (Visions of the Sleeping Bard)* des walisischen Autors

---

01 „CERITH WYN EVANS IN CONVERSATION WITH JAN VERWOERT", IN: KATALOG ZUR AUSSTELLUNG *FURTHER – ARTISTS FROM WALES*. 50. VENEDIG BIENNALE. S. 70-85.

Ellis Wynne von 1703 handeln würde, einem Klassiker der walisischen Literatur, der das ekstatische Erlebnis eines Dichters beschreibt, der von Engeln in den Himmel getragen wird und die gesamte Welt aus der Luft betrachtet (um gerade in Venedig den größten Sündenpfuhl auf Erden zu erblicken). Ich war zudem darüber aufgeklärt, dass die Idee und Handlung von Wynnes Buch auf dem Buch *Sueños y Discursos (Dreams and Discourses)* des spanischen Autros Francisco de Quevedo von 1627 basiert, dessen Text wiederum zeitgleich in der Ausstellung *Utopia Station* in den Arsenalen von Venedig von einer einfachen Lampe gemorst werden würde. Auf der konzeptuellen Ebene hatte ich also bereits eine klare Vorstellung von der Aussage der beiden in geisterhaftem Dialog miteinander verbundenen Morsesignale: ein Bekenntnis zu der utopischen Kraft ekstatischer Erfahrungen, die bestehende Ordnung der Welt zu transzendieren und einen Raum zu eröffnen, in dem Texte, deren Stimmen nicht mehr an konkrete Subjekte gebunden sind, in einer Kommunikation aufeinander bezogen werden, der Raum und Zeit überbrückt und der Fantasie einer autonomen Sphäre Gestalt verleiht, in der zwei Texte ohne menschliches Einwirken miteinander kommunizieren.

Ich hatte davon gehört, dass ein Testlauf der Apparatur für den Abend vor der Eröffnung der Biennale vorgesehen war, diese Information aber umgehend vergessen, war nachts auf der Straße unterwegs und mit Freunden im Gespräch und hatte eigentlich nur durch Zufall nach oben geschaut, um dann den weithin über allen Dächern der Stadt sichtbaren, schnurgerade in den Nachthimmel hineingezeichneten Lichtstrahl zu sehen, der just in diesem Augenblick kurz verlosch, um erneut aufzuleuchten, als ob er mir mit einem Zwinkern zu verstehen geben wollte, dass er zur Kenntnis nimmt, dass ich ihn zur Kenntnis nehme. In diesem Moment musste ich feststellen, dass mein gesamtes Vorwissen mich in keiner Form auf die Erfahrung vorbereitet hatte, die Arbeit realisiert zu sehen. Der konzeptuelle Horizont der Arbeit war für den Augenblick zusammengeschmolzen zu dem Gefühl: „Das ist es jetzt". Und dieses Gefühl war auf überraschende Weise vollkommen euphorisch. Diese Euphorie ähnelte dem Triumphgefühl, das einen beim Anblick architektonischer Wunderwerke überkommen mag, die der Schwerkraft trotzen und so das Gefühl einer Freiheit vermitteln, die sich durch keine Gesetze, und erst Recht nicht die der Natur, binden lässt – das Gefühl: „Und es geht doch!"

Wesentlich für die Intensität dieser Erfahrung war dabei aber das Gefühl, von dem Lichtsignal zum Zeugen einer erhabenen Unverschämtheit gemacht zu werden. Der erste Gedanke war: Mit welchem Recht kann sich jemand herausnehmen, etwas so Schönes zu produzieren? Eine in ihrer Einfachheit erhabene Form, die sich in ihrer Einfachheit aber nicht genügt, sondern beginnt, mit mir zu kommunizieren, und das auf eine überraschend intime Weise. Das gemorste Signal wird zum Innuendo. Der monumentale Lichtstrahl scheint mir zuzublinzeln. (Wie eine Diva, die von der Bühne herab einer Person im Publikum einen Blick zuwirft.) Dieses Zublinzeln macht mich zum Mitwisser eines Aktes, der allein durch die Inszenierung eines erhabenen Spektakels und damit der schamlosen Behauptung: Hier, das ist schön. Das weißt und willst Du doch auch, oder?

Die unerwartete Intimität des Gefühls, von dem Lichtstrahl angesprochen zu werden, war jedoch unmittelbar begleitet von dem Wissen, dass nicht nur ich dieses Signal gerade wahrnehme, sondern dass dieses Signal weithin sichtbar ist, dass also potenziell jeder, der jetzt in Venedig und Umgebung in den Nachthimmel schaut, sich von dem aufblinkenden Lichtstrahl angesprochen fühlen könnte, dass aber wahrscheinlich wie ich niemand in der Lage sein würde, dieses Signal zu decodieren – es sei denn, irgendwo in Venedig fände sich jemand, der sowohl den Morsecode als auch Walisisch beherrscht. Allein diese Vorstellung setzt bereits eine neue Assoziationskette in Gang: Wer wäre der ideale Empfänger des Signals, wenn nicht eine Figur wie aus einem Roman des 19. Jahrhunderts (ein walisischer Weltreisender zur See zum Beispiel, der, aus einem Grund, zu dessen Erklärung wiederum das Erzählen einer langen Geschichte nötig wäre, zurzeit in Venedig residiert)? Auf diese Weise multipliziert sich die Anzahl der potenziellen Adressaten der Arbeit. Mit wem kommuniziert der Lichtstrahl? Mit mir? Mit allen? Nur mit sich selbst? Oder mit einem anderen Sender, einer Lampe in den Arsenalen, die einen zweiten Text morst? Dadurch, dass ein wesentliches Moment von *Cleave 03*, die Frage nach dem potenziellen Adressaten der Arbeit, auf entschiedene Weise unentschieden bleibt, enthüllt die Arbeit ihren spekulativen Charakter. Der Adressat wird von einer Realität zu einem Potenzial. Dasselbe gilt für die Konzeption der Arbeit. Das Faktum der realisierten Arbeit verändert den Status des Konzeptes grundlegend. Vor der Erfahrung der Realisierung ist das Konzept Teil eines Wissens, das man für eine Erklärung, Begründung oder Rechtfertigung der Arbeit halten könnte. Im Moment der Erfahrung jedoch zeigt sich, dass die Arbeit nicht durch ihr Konzept erklärt, begründet oder gerechtfertigt wird. Ihre einzige Legitimation ist ihre Existenz, das Faktum der realisierten Geste. Die Tatsache, dass der Lichtstrahl umwerfend schön ist, ist Rechtfertigung genug. Dass dem Konzept der Status einer Begründung entzogen wird, bedeutet nun aber nicht, dass das Konzept für obsolet erklärt wird. Im Gegenteil, es wird aufgewertet, weil es von einer klaren Funktion entbunden und freigestellt wird – die Konzeption der Arbeit wird angesichts des Faktums der realisierten Arbeit in einen Horizont möglicher Fragen transformiert, die sich in Bezug auf die Arbeit stellen: In welchem Verhältnis könnten die Geschichte der Texte und Personen Wynne und de Quevedo zueinander und zum kulturellen Phänomen des Morsecodes stehen? Wer spricht hier mit wem in welcher Sprache über was? Und vor allem: Welche Sprache, welches Wissen und welche Erfahrungsdimension werden durch eine Kommunikation konstituiert, die sich zugleich an mich, an alle und an keinen richtet? Wem sagt eine Sprache etwas, die sich selbst spricht, die mit sich selbst spricht, weil sie kaum mehr jemand spricht, obwohl sie in ihrer Signalwirkung alle anspricht?

Der entscheidende spekulative Zug der Arbeit zeigt sich so in der Art und Weise, wie sie den Status des Wissens, das ihr zu Grunde liegt, verändert. Man könnte sagen: *Cleave 03* verdreht die Position des

Wissens in der Zeit im Verhältnis zum Zeitpunkt der Realisierung. Die Spekulation dreht die Zeit um ihre eigene Achse. Während das Wissen vor der Erfahrung der realisierten Arbeit als etwas aufgefasst werden konnte, das der Arbeit in Form einer Konzeption, Begründung oder Rechtfertigung *vorausgeht*, so wird das Wissen nun als etwas erfahrbar, das überhaupt erst von der Arbeit hervorgebracht werden könnte, als etwas, das von der Arbeit *ausgeht* und in Frageform in die Zukunft projiziert wird, als ein *potenzielles* und nicht ein *reelles* Wissen: Was die Arbeit weiß, weiß jetzt noch niemand. Es handelt sich um ein Wissen, das erst in Zukunft durch die Beantwortung der Fragen produziert werden kann, die die Arbeit aufwirft – und das auch nicht mit absoluter Sicherheit, schließlich lässt sich nicht ausschließen, dass es sich bei den Fluchtlinien, die die Arbeit für ein zukünftiges Denken entwirft, nicht um falsche Fährten handelt.

MODELL: DIE POTENZIALE VON FELDERN

Die Erfahrung der Arbeit *Cleave 03* ist also dadurch gekennzeichnet, dass sie (im wahrsten Sinne des Wortes) eine Projektion von noch zu denkenden Gedanken ist. Der Gegenstand der Erfahrung sind Potenziale. Deswegen drängt die Erfahrung, selbst wenn sie sich in ihrer eigenen Schönheit auch genügen könnte, von sich aus über sich hinaus auf eine Abstraktion ihrer selbst. Die Erfahrung ist materiell in der Realität verankert (die Projektion war aus technischen Gründen nur eine Woche lang an diesem Ort zu sehen). Dennoch besitzt sie einen Modellstatus. Sie behauptet sich als Modell einer anderen Sprache, eines zukünftigen Wissens und einer Erfahrung, die zugleich konkret und abstrakt ist. Aus diesem Grund scheint es berechtigt zu sein, von der Erfahrung wieder zu abstrahieren und ihren Modellcharakter zu beschreiben: Dass das Denken in Modellen ein Grundzug spekulativen Denkens ist, macht die Lektüre der Texte von Gilles Deleuze deutlich. Hier findet sich ein Denken, das mit einer lustvollen Dreistigkeit fremden Diskursen Metaphern entnimmt und zu gültigen philosophischen Modellen ausbaut. Die Modelle von Deleuze verdeutlichen die Bedeutung spekulativen Denkens dabei auf eine zweifache Weise: Zum einen sind sie Versuche einer Beschreibung dessen, was spekulatives Denken ausmacht. Zum anderen aber sind sie die ureigenste Ausdrucksform dieses spekulativen Denkens, das sich dadurch vollzieht, dass es imaginative Modelle davon entwirft, was es sein könnte. Ein Modell, das in Bezug auf die Arbeit von Cerith Wyn Evans interessant erscheint, ist die von Deleuze aus der Mathematik und Physik entlehnte Metaphorik der Potenzialitäten. In der Differentialrechnung bezeichnet der Begriff der „Potenz" offenbar (das heißt: wenn ich es richtig verstehe) den Differentialquotienten. Deleuze erklärt: „Die Potenz ist die Form der Wechselbestimmung, der zufolge variable Größen als Funktionen von einander begriffen werden; ..."[02] In der Funktionsrechnung lässt sich anhand des Verhältnisses der variablen Größen eines Differentials, der Potenz, der Verlauf einer Kurve, einer Bewegung also, beschreiben, die, so deutet es Deleuze, in jedem ihrer Punkte dennoch einzigartig ist. Es geht Deleuze hier um die Identifikation eines Prinzips, das die Kontinuität einer Bewegung beschreibt, die in jedem Stadium ihres virtuellen Fortschreitens immer wieder neue Singularitäten hervorbringt. Dieses Prinzip ist eine bestimmte Differenz, ein definiertes Verhältnis zwischen zwei variablen Größen, das als Potenzial zum Motor einer Bewegung wird. In der Physik wiederum wird das Kräftepotenzial, das allein aus dem spezifischen Verhältnis zweier Objekte zueinander entsteht, als „Lageenergie" bezeichnet (die Energie, die ein Objekt dadurch erhält, dass seine Position im Verhältnis zu anderen Objekten verändert wird, zum Beispiel, indem es hochgehoben und so in die Lage versetzt wird, im Fall „Arbeit" zu verrichten). Allein durch die Bestimmung eines wechselseitigen Verhältnisses innerhalb eines Feldes von Objekten baut sich in diesem Feld eine potenzielle Energie auf. Deleuze nennt diese Energie „Intensität".[03]

Die Konstruktion dieses Modells hat (mindestens) zwei Pointen in Bezug auf eine Bestimmung dessen, was spekulatives Denken ausmacht.

---

[02] GILLES DELEUZE: *DIFFERENZ UND WIEDERHOLUNG*, MÜNCHEN 1992, S. 224.

Erstens: Das Potenzial spekulativen Denkens liegt darin, dass es Dinge und Begriffe auf unerwartete Art und Weise in ein Verhältnis zueinander setzt und sie dadurch in Bewegung bringt und in die Lage versetzt, Arbeit zu verrichten und etwas Singuläres hervorzubringen. Zweitens: Die Kraft, die das Denken hervorbringt, ist keine Kraft, die durch ein Subjekt ausgeübt wird. Es sind vielmehr die Verhältnisse selbst, die das Denken konstruiert, die diese Kraft erzeugen. Das Denken produziert ein Feld, aus dessen differentieller Struktur sich alle weiteren Entwicklungen von selbst ergeben. Das Feld ist das Subjekt der Potenzialitäten. Interessanterweise operiert auch die aktuelle Parapsychologie mit einem vergleichbaren Modell aus der Quantenphysik. Hier wird beobachtet, dass in geschlossenen Systemen Elemente in ein Verhältnis zueinander treten, Energien generieren und Prozesse auslösen können, ohne dass sie in direktem physischen Kontakt miteinander stehen müssten. Man spricht von „nichtlokalen Korrelationen". Wenn im Zuge einer Séance zum Beispiel Objekte in Bewegung geraten oder ein Medium Dinge wahrnimmt, die an einem anderen Ort stattfinden, so erklärt man sich dies als „nichtlokale Korrelation": Innerhalb eines bestimmten Feldes stimmen sich verschiedene Prozesse so aufeinander ein, dass ihre strukturelle Kommunikation aktuelle Ergebnisse hervorbringt.[04]

Im Prinzip lassen sich die aktuellen Installationen von Cerith Wyn Evans anhand dieses Modells als Felder von Potenzialitäten beschreiben. Die eigentliche künstlerische Geste besteht darin, ein Feld dadurch herzustellen, dass verschiedene Dinge in ein Verhältnis zueinander gesetzt werden, mit dem Ziel, dass dieses Feld daraufhin aus seiner eigenen Dynamik heraus Potenziale aufbaut, Intensitäten erzeugt und unerwartete Prozesse in Bewegung setzt. Es geht um die Herstellung eines Feldes, das arbeitet. Dass den subjektlosen Dynamiken, die

---

03 EBD., S. 294.

04 SIEHE HIERZU WALTER VON LUCADOU IM VORWORT ZU DERS.: *DIMENSION PSI – FAKTEN ZUR PARAPSYCHOLOGIE*, O.O. 2003.

dieses Feld aufgrund seiner Potenziale in Gang setzt, der geisterhafte Charakter von Prozessen, die im Rahmen einer Séance stattfinden könnten, ähnelt, ist somit kein Zufall. (Ebenso wenig ist es ein Zufall, dass, kurz nachdem Samuel Morse 1844 sein erstes Telegramm im Morsecode versandte, bereits 1847 die Töchter der Methodistenfamilie Fox in Hydesville bei New York Klopfzeichen von Geistern aus den Mauern ihres Hauses empfingen und beantworteten und so den modernen Spiritismus begründeten.[05] Mit der Geschichte der modernen medialen Kommunikation verbinden sich von Anfang an Berichte über geisterhafte Vorkommnisse und unvorhergesehene Interferenzen.)

Die Installation *Look at this picture...How does it appear to you now? Does it seem to be persisting?* (2003) ist ein solches Feld, das arbeitet. Sie stellt ein Verhältnis her zwischen einer Serie von Objekten, Diskursen und Personen. Fünf verschiedene Texte werden durch Computer fortlaufend in Morsecode übersetzt. Die codierten Signale werden daraufhin durch fünf verschiedene Kronleuchter übertragen, deren Glühlampen der Frequenz des Signals entsprechend aufleuchten und verglimmen. Die Leuchter wirken prachtvoll. Sie sind überwiegend aus Glas gefertigt, unterscheiden sich in ihrer Form jedoch stark voneinander. So entsteht der Eindruck, dass jeder Leuchter dem Text, den er überträgt, eine individuell verschiedene sinnliche Erscheinungsform, eine besondere theatrale Präsenz gibt. Auf fünf Flachbildschirmen an der Stirnwand des Installationsraumes lässt sich der automatisierte Chiffrierungsprozess nachvollziehen. Die zum gegebenen Zeitpunkt gesendete Textpassage erscheint hier parallel zur grafischen Notierung des Morsecodes.

Ein Leuchter mit zwölf geschwungenen Armen, hergestellt von Barovier & Toso, überträgt das Interview „Goodnight Eileen" (1982) von Terry Wilson mit Brion Gysin, der von seinen Erinnerungen an das Medium

---

[05] SIEHE HIERZU MICHAEL KRAJEWSKI: „MEDIUMISTISCHE WESEN ALS KÜNSTLER", IN: *KUNSTFORUM INTERNATIONAL*, NR. 163. JAN.-FEB. 2003, S. 56.

Eileen Garrett erzählt, die aufgrund ihrer Prognose eines militärischen Unfalls erst verhaftet wurde, um dann für die CIA zu arbeiten. Eine Lampe in funktionalistischem Design aus kugelförmig angeordneten Glühbirnen, hergestellt von Achille Castiglione, überträgt den Roman *La Princesse de Clèves* (1678), eine multi-perspektivisch organisierte Erzählung über die romantische Liebe, die vermutlich von verschiedenen Mitgliedern des Salons der Madame de Lafayette verfasst wurde. Ein aus dünnen Glasstäben zusammengesetzter großer, rundlicher Leuchter, hergestellt von Venini Quadratti, überträgt assoziative Aphorismen von John Cage mit dem Titel „Diary: How to Improve the World (You Will Only Make Matters Worse) Continued 1968 (Revised)". Ein Leuchter aus gläsernen Blütenkelchen, hergestellt von Galliano Ferro, überträgt den Aufsatz „Paranoid reading and reparative reading, or, you're so paranoid, you probably think this essay is about you" (2003) von Eve Kosofsky Sedgwick, theoretische Reflektionen über die imaginäre Positionierung des Lesers in einem Text beim Lesen. Ein festlicher, vermutlich für den Palais des Beaux Arts in Brüssel entworfener Leuchter mit dem Namen Lustre Marie-Terese überträgt den Essay „The Stars Down to Earth" (1957) von Theodor W. Adorno, eine kritische Analyse des modernen Spiritismus als systemkonforme Einwilligung in das Gefühl der Fremdbestimmung und die Verdinglichung des Denkens.

Die Notwendigkeit einer derart ausführlichen Beschreibung macht den Grad der Genauigkeit deutlich, mit der die Bestandteile der Installation im Detail definiert sind. Die Spannung, die die Arbeit als Feld aufbaut, liegt nun aber gerade darin, dass diese für sich genommen klar bestimmbaren Elemente in einem Verhältnis aufeinander bezogen werden, das auf entschiedene Weise unentschieden ist. Natürlich ist es grundsätzlich möglich, sich in dem Feld, das die Installation eröffnet, zu orientieren, wenn man es als Diskurs begreift und die Leuchter und ihre Signale den verschiedenen Texten und Autoren zuordnet und diese dann wiederum mit bestimmten Traditionen des Denkens identifiziert: In diesem Sinne könnte man sagen, dass die Arbeit eine

Konfrontation zwischen einer Schule des analytisch kritischen Denkens und einer Schule des spekulativ ekstatisch entgrenzenden Denkens inszeniert. Aber über die spezifischen Effekte, die das Zusammenwirken der hier versammelten Diskurse erzeugt, ist damit noch ebenso wenig gesagt wie über das Verhältnis, das ich als Rezipient dieser Arbeit zu diesen Diskursen eingehe. Wie reagieren die Komponenten miteinander? Auf welcher Ebene kommunizieren sie überhaupt miteinander und mit mir? Auf der Ebene eines inhaltlichen Diskurses oder auf der Ebene einer rein ästhetischen Erfahrung? Obwohl alle Elemente der Inszenierung bestimmbar sind, bleibt doch offen, um was für eine Art von Szenarium es sich hier handelt. In dieser Offenheit liegt das Spannungspotenzial, das die Installation als Feld erzeugt.

Die Arbeit, die dieses Feld verrichtet, lässt sich zunächst als ein Prozessieren von Wissen beschreiben, das mich als Betrachter in ein anderes Verhältnis zu diesem Wissen setzt. Die eigendynamische Arbeit des Feldes entbindet mich von der Pflicht, wissen zu müssen. Das Wissen prozessieren bereits die Computer. Sie erledigen die Arbeit der Vergegenwärtigung des Wissens automatisch. Der Diskurs vollzieht sich vollautomatisiert. Die Anforderungen der Didaktik, Kunst als Bildung zu erschließen durch eine Aneignung und Verinnerlichung ihres Wissens, sind dadurch aufgehoben. Die Automaten erfüllen das Pflichtprogramm. Mir bleibt das Vergnügen, mich dem vermittelten Wissen mit einer luxuriös verantwortungslosen „interpassiven" Einstellung nähern zu können. Wenn sich der Diskurs als subjektlos fließender Strom von Signalen vermittelt, die von verschwenderisch schönen Kronleuchtern übertragen werden, was bleibt mir da anderes übrig als mich diesem Strom zu überlassen? Die angemessene Reaktion auf den Prozess, den die Arbeit als Feld in Gang setzt, ist, sich auf die Atmosphäre, die sie erzeugt, einzustimmen und sich gehen zu lassen. Tune in und Drop out. Das ist das Protokoll, das ich befolgen muss, um das Potenzial der Arbeit in der Erfahrung zu erschließen. Diese Erfahrung ähnelt der einer Séance: Die Rätselhaftigkeit der Leuchtsignale und die auratische Dinghaftigkeit der Leuchter vermitteln das Gefühl der geisterhaften Präsenz der versammelten, lebenden wie toten Autoren in einem Raum.

Nachdem die Bedeutung des Wissens zunächst durch seine Automatisierung aufgehoben wird, so rekonstituiert sich diese Bedeutung nun auf unerwartete Weise auf einer neuen Ebene. Die Bedeutung des Diskurses manifestiert sich in den Signalen der Leuchter als gestaltloses aber dennoch personifiziertes Denken. Wenn ich zum Beispiel die Signale von Adornos Leuchter verfolge, dann kann ich mich des Eindrucks nicht erwehren, dass da jemand mit mir spricht. Der Geist von Adorno materialisiert sich vor meinen Augen im Aufglühen und besonders im Verglimmen der Lichter, die nie ganz verlöschen, bevor sie wieder aufleuchten und so unwillkürlich an das Ausatmen eines Menschen erinnern, das auch nie zum Stillstand führt, sondern den Anfang einer neuen Atembewegung markiert. Mit gläubiger Ergriffenheit hat diese Erfahrung jedoch nichts zu tun. Schließlich ist die Botschaft dieses Geistes eine virtuos spöttische Zurückweisung des spiritistischen Irrglaubens. Das Phantom des Autors verpflichtet mich auf den Geist seines Textes, und das ist der Geist der Kritik, man könnte auch sagen: das kritische Potenzial des Textes. Mit anderen Worten: Die Atmosphäre der Arbeit lässt mich Kritik *als Potenzial* erfahren.

Die Erfahrung einer von auratischen Leuchtern durch Leuchtsignale vermittelten geisterhaften Präsenz von Texten und ihren Autoren ist die Erfahrung von intellektuellen Potenzialen. Diese Erfahrung von Potenzialität ist nicht in sich abgeschlossen. Sie stellt sich nicht mit der Gewissheit eines Erlebnisses im Hier und Jetzt ein. Das entscheidende Moment dieser Erfahrung (das sie der Erfahrung einer Séance ähneln lässt) ist ja gerade die Auflösung der Einheit von Zeit und Raum: Die versammelten Diskurse und Autoren entstammen verschiedenen Zeiten und kulturellen Räumen. Diese Differenzen hebt ihre Zusammenkunft nicht auf. Ihr zeitliches Verhältnis zueinander ist die Gleichzeitigkeit des Ungleichzeitigen, ihr räumliches die „nichtlokale Korrelation". Die historischen Koordinaten des Zeitfensters, in dem sich die Geister der Texte und Autoren begegnen, sind ebenso unentschieden wie die räumlichen Koordinaten ihrer Nähe und Distanz. Sind diese Autoren schon miteinander in Berührung gekommen? Nehmen sie in ihren Texte aufeinander Bezug? Ist ihre Beziehung bereits Geschichte? Oder begegnen sie sich jetzt hier zum ersten Mal? Hat sich das intellektuelle Potenzial, das in ihrer Begegnung steckt, schon entladen, oder baut es sich gerade erst auf? Stehen sich diese Autoren nahe oder bleiben sie sich in ihrem Denken fremd? In welchem Verhältnis die einberufenen Geister zueinander stehen, bleibt unentscheidbar. Sicher ist nur, dass dieses Verhältnis intensiv ist: Sie senden einander ununterbrochen Signale. Das kann man sehen. Zum einen ist ihre Beziehung also spekulativ als reine Möglichkeit zu denken. Zum anderen ist ihre Beziehung aber auch in der Installation als sinnlich erfahrbare Wirklichkeit zu erleben.

Dieses Paradox erschließt den Kern der Erfahrung von Potenzialität, die die Installation herstellt: Es ist die Erfahrung realer Virtualitäten. Die Beziehung der Geister der im Raum versammelten Autoren ist real und virtuell zugleich. Der Diskurs zwischen ihnen ist historisch möglich, er ist ein Potenzial der Geschichte des Denkens. Dieses geschichtliche Potenzial ist jedoch keine historische Tatsache. Die Arbeit erzeugt es ja überhaupt erst in der Gegenwart. Die historische Bedeutung dieses Potenzials lässt sich daher erst im Rahmen ihrer möglichen Rezeption, und das heißt in der Zukunft, ermessen. Ebenso wie *Cleave 03* verschiebt *Look at this picture...How does it appear to you now? Does it seem to be persisting?* den Ort der Bedeutung in der Zeit aus der Geschichte des ratifizierten Wissens in die Zukunft eines spekulativen Denkens. Indem er das Potenzial von Denken und das Potenzial einer Beziehung zwischen verschiedenen Formen des Denkens als reale Virtualiät erfahrbar macht, entspricht Cerith Wyn Evans einem zentralen Anliegen spekulativen Denkens: das Verhältnis zwischen Möglichem und Wirklichem nicht als Unterschied sondern als paradoxe Gleichzeitigkeit aufzufassen. Von seinen Arbeiten zu sagen, dass sie reale Virtualitäten inszenieren, bedeutet: Hier ist alles so, wie es wäre, wenn es wäre, wie es ist. Über das utopische Potenzial, das dieser Auffassung innewohnt, ist damit noch fast gar nichts gesagt.

JULIANE REBENTISCH
DECOLONIZED THEATER

IN THEATRICAL ILLEGIBILITY, IN THE NIGHT THAT PRECEDES THE BOOK, THE SIGN HAS NOT YET BEEN SEPARATED FROM FORCE. IT IS NOT QUITE YET A SIGN, IN THE SENSE IN WHICH WE UNDERSTAND SIGN, BUT IT IS NO LONGER A *THING*, WHICH WE CONCEIVE ONLY AS OPPOSED TO THE SIGN. IT HAS, THEN, NO CHANCE TO BECOME, IN THIS STATE, A WRITTEN TEXT OR AN ARTICULATED SPEECH; NO CHANCE TO RISE AND TO INFLATE ITSELF ABOVE *ENERGEIA* IN ORDER TO BE INVESTED ... WITH THE SOMBER AND OBJECTIVE IMPASSIVITY OF THE *ERGON*.[01] (JACQUES DERRIDA)

Opening Night in the Frankfurter Kunstverein: downstairs, social activities, loosely grouped around the figure of the artist; upstairs, everyone left alone with the scenes that he has staged "for us," for his audience, only to dissolve any possible collectivity in them immediately. If Cerith Wyn Evans's installations can be described as theater, then it is a theater that can only be attended alone, a theater that does not reveal itself by attending it but instead expects the individual to make it happen. No curtain is drawn back; everything is there already when one steps in; and everything remains there when the one leaves the scenes again at some vigourously arbitrary moment. For what happens inside has no measurable performance time that experience could seize upon; there is no objective end here, after which one can relax and turn away with a casual, confident "done that." And there is no dramatic event that could guide our attention to the goal of understanding by following the lines of a story or an allegorical meaning. Nevertheless, it is something like theater.

A theater of signs and things, for example, as in one of the upstairs exhibition spaces, whose otherwise quite neutral atmosphere is now superimposed with the melancholy of an abandoned ballroom enlivened with the relics of lost worlds. Even this livening up of the room with objects has an evident theatrical quality to it, since it is taken quite literally here: five different chandeliers reign supreme in the room, each in its own individual opulence; their lights go on and off at irregular

---

01 JACQUES DERRIDA, "LA PAROLE SOUFFLÉE," IN IDEM, *WRITING AND DIFFERENCE*, TRANS. ALAN BASS (CHICAGO: UNIV. OF CHICAGO PRESS, 1978), 169-95, ESP. 189.

intervals, sending signals – Morse code, it as it turns out. Each chandelier transmits a different text. On the flat screens installed discreetly on the wall the texts appear at the same speed as their translation – or performance – by this impressive play of lights that lies behind us with its silent polyphony of light and dark when we turn to begin reading the texts in the constant bluish light of the monitors. As if we were trying to identify the actors with their roles during a theatrical performance by studying the program, we try to associate the chandeliers with their texts. What a constellation! A classically elegant Barovier & Torso chandelier "speaks" a text from a volume of interviews with Brion Gysin – an artist, writer, and comrade-in-arms of William S. Burroughs – in which he describes his encounter with the professional medium Eileen Garrett. A modern, compactly round chandelier by Achille Castiglione transmits an excerpt from the novel *La princesse de Clèves*, which was probably written in collaboration by several members of Madame de Lafayette's salon. It is the earliest literary document of the concept of romantic love. Excerpts from the collected writings of John Cage are performed by an object by Venini Quadratti, which looks more like fireworks than a lamp. A longish model with playful floral motifs by Galliano Ferro translates literary scholar and queer studies theorist Eve Kosofsky Sedgwick's reflections on the paranoid tendencies inherent in the experience of reading a text that seems to build the reader's position into it. And finally an antique chandelier transmits to us a small excerpt from Theodor W. Adorno's "The Stars Down to Earth," a socio-psychological study of an astrology column in *The Los Angeles Times*.

Arranged as they are, the five chandeliers potentially represent not only their quite varied texts but also their respective authors. At times, particularly in the afterglow of the bulbs in semidarkness, they take on an almost anthropomorphic quality; they become mediums less in the technological than in the occult sense. Nevertheless, the slightly uncanny effect of their spectacle does not resolve into the allusions that can be made on the semantic level between early media theories and the parapsychological abilities of glamorous Eileen Garrett. Rather, it exists much more fundamentally in the *latency* of such anthropomorphic qualities beneath the material objecthood of the chandeliers. In other words, it lies in the fact that these everyday objects, however luxurious they might be, are capable of taking on quasi-subjective features at all. For this is never openly demonstrated. It was in precisely such *masked* anthropomorphism that Michael Fried, in his infamous 1967 article on the provocatively simple objects of Minimal Art saw a crucial aspect of what he called, with pejorative intent, their "theatricality."[02] What the simple objects of Minimal Art share with the far from simple chandeliers that Cerith Wyn Evans cast in his production, is their theatrical double presence: a chair on the stage is always at once a simple chair and a symbol of something else – Lear's throne, say; an actor onstage always simultaneous presents himself and something else: the character in the drama. In contrast, however, to traditional dramatic theater, in which the actors and the stage props are meant to make the dramatic world they are presenting as transparent as possible, and the level of representation is meant to step back behind the represented, in this chandelier installation the theatrical tension between representation and represented is left decidedly unresolved.

We are confronted here with a *mise en scène* that lacks a genuine drama, with a theater that has been decolonized of the despotism of drama, as it were. There is, admittedly a text here too, but it literally appears *alongside* the other means of representation – and thus it comes to the fore as another such means. Character by character, the text appears slowly on the monitors and thus becomes partially autonomous relative to its corresponding signified. Moreover, the text obtains a rather abstract relationship to the light signals that encode it; for, despite the suggestion of their readability, the latter are

---

[02] MICHAEL FRIED, "ART AND OBJECTHOOD," IN IDEM, *ART AND OBJECTHOOD: ESSAYS AND REVIEWS* (CHICAGO: UNIV. OF CHICAGO PRESS, 1996).

unreadable for most of us. The dimension of representation does not become transparent relative to what's possibly represented; rather, representation and represented enter into a relationship of tension that cannot be resolved on any pole, neither that of the material or technological facticity of the chandeliers nor that of a particular textual meaning. Each pole exists for us only in its conflicting relationship to the other. The fact that the chandeliers are removed from their inconspicuous familiarity of their usual functional context draws attention to their glassy, electrical mediality; but this does not present itself to us in a positivistic way, as a mere sense datum, but in and through its tense relation to an open horizon of possible meanings. The relation is a tense one because the dimensions of meaning that the intertextual web of Gysin, Madame de Lafayette, Cage, Sedgwick, and Adorno might produce can never be objectively tied to the chandeliers but merely appear on them – for a moment, like the brief intervals of the Morse code – only to drop back a moment later, noncommittally, into the appealing play of light on the blinking surfaces wich opens up possibilities for new semantic formations.

The stage presence of these chandeliers derives not from embodying or symbolizing a particular thing (a text, a person, a meaning in the media, literature, art, or social theories) but rather from involving us, each of us, in a process in which our production of meaning necessarily proves in the end to have been a projection, only to be sparked again by their potential of representation. Indeed, here we are in the work (Sedgwick);[03] it exists only for us – only in the course of our ultimately unstoppable process of understanding is the work put to work, liberated as an artwork. The stage presence of the chandeliers, their aesthetic quality, unfolds through an essentially individual experience in which the relationship of tension between thing and sign is

---

[03] EVE KOSOFSKY SEDGWICK, "PARANOID READING AND REPARATIVE READING; OR, YOU'RE SO PARANOID, YOU PROBABLY THINK THIS ESSAY IS ABOUT YOU," IN IDEM, *TOUCHING FEELING: AFFECT, PEDAGOGY, PERFORMATIVITY* (DURHAM, NC: DUKE UNIV. PRESS, 2003),123-151.

played out. What takes place in this work plays out in the nocturnal area of the "no longer" and the "not yet" (Derrida) that evidently escapes the categories of modernist aesthetic theories, oriented as they are around objectivity independent of viewer and context. The process we enter here, in this installation, can neither be objectively attached to the texts or objects assembled in it nor subjectively ascribed entirely to the imaginative capacity of the viewer. *Look at That Picture...* , Wyn Evans entitles his installation, *How Does It Appear to You Now? Does It Seem to Be Persisting?* The meanings that *appear* in one way or another in his work are neither simply to be objectively discovered there nor read into them deliberately by us. We experience ourselves here as performative, as productive, but without being able to bring the corresponding forces under our control entirely.

But that which can be described from the objectivist perspective of modernist aesthetic theories – like that of Michael Fried, say, the critic of theatricality – only as a loss of control and alienation (from both the object and oneself), could also, critically evoking the Kantian tradition, be called pleasure: the self-reflexive experience of the developing of subjective powers in and through the relation to an aesthetic object. On the object's side, this experience is mirrored in the concept of aesthetic semblance. For semblance in the post-Kantian tradition of philosophical aesthetics can be referred to as the "nonautonomous become autonomous" – as which we must understand aesthetic experience in its performance, or productivity.[04] The performativity of aesthetic experience would thus be understood not in the sense of the carrying out of an action but in the sense of an event *between* subject and object that rather happens to the experiencing subject than it is something he or she intentionally carries out. This is an experience that can be translated directly neither into cognition nor into action; an experience, therefore, that on the basis of its specific logic

---

[04] RÜDIGER BUBNER, *ÄSTHETISCHE ERFAHRUNG* (FRANKFURT AM MAIN: SUHRKAMP, 1989), 39.

– the specific logic of the aesthetic – occupies an autonomous area with regard to the spheres of theoretical and practical reason. In this sense, theatrical art in the tradition of Minimal Art is particularly suited to bringing out the features of aesthetic experience that had previously been marginalized by modernist aesthetic theories: their self-reflective and performative quality as well as their essential endlessness.

This intertwined correspondence between the work and its viewer, in which a certain association of meaning can suddenly occupy the center of aesthetic significance, only to withdraw again in the next moment as a merely external projection, and with that give rise to potentially endless new associations, finds its theoretical image, as it were, in the Frankfurt exhibition itself. In another room hangs, in the form of convoluted neon tubes, the stylized depiction of the *Moebius Strip* (1997), which is, famously, twisted in such a way that one can move from its outside to its inside without crossing an edge. But even this kind of metaaesthetic reading is nothing but a projection, *semblance*. Once again its nocturnal work is not denied in favor of a supposed objectivity of the "genuine work" but reflected on spatially. Next to *Slow Fade to Black (Reversed)*, a neon sign that is installed on the ceiling in mirror reverse, so that it can be read in the window opposite it, the mirror reflection of *Moebius Strip* in that same window, appears, for a moment, to be the true center of the work; and the brutalist building that one sees when looking out of the Kunstverein to be part of the work. In *Slow Fade to Black (Reversed)* the staging of outside on the inside and inside on the outside – the reversible sliding of meanings on the edge between the two – obtains a clearly cinematic quality. The concrete architecture framed in the window in Cinemascope format looks like a film still; the neon sign is like a subtitle that calls attention to the filmic process in a Brechtian way, announcing that the image will soon have resolved into black. This does not happen, of course; the final image stops short just before it resolves, strangely hovering, and thus transforms into a kind of duration piece, which sneakily foists the tension of Hitchcock's *Rear*

Window onto the small changes in light relationships in the space outside. Just as Wyn Evans's procedures decidedly remove the plot from theater, so they do from film as well, which in many respects, thanks to its heightened potential for illusion, has taken over the functions of traditional dramatic theater. There is clearly neither a dramatic event nor a story here, nor even a film projection at all, just the casual reflection of a neon sign in the window. If there is a projection here, it is simply that of the viewers, who are caught up in the semantic loops that spin between them and the work, infinitely connecting outside and inside.

Wyn Evans isolates the viewer's performative-projective activity in another way in an installation that is cinematic in the broadest sense: *Dreamachine*. In the middle of a Japanese-style interior surrounded by palms, a cylindrical lampshade pierced with holes is turning on a minimalist base and casting floating points of light into a room that is otherwise rather dark. Looking directly at the light machine with closed eyes, one senses dynamic, bright colorful dots, patterns even, on the retina. Based on a design by Brion Gysin and Ian Sommerville that dates back to the 1960s, *Dreamachine* thus realizes, in a very direct, almost literal way, the idea of a kind of "cinema in the head" whose imaginative energies were supposed to be mobilized by the expanded cinema of that area against the intellectual passivity to which the immersive illusionism of the commercial dream factory condemns its public. It isn't necessary to know that Wyn Evans has a background in experimental film to see that he has remained committed to that critical project. It is continued here in several respects. For example, the dots of light that *Dreamachine* places before our inner eye have a pendant adjacent that externalizes the same experience, as it were. A beamer mounted on the ceiling projects a cone of light onto the wall, and its round white contains nothing but light colored dots; now and again, as the only "cinematic" effect, a dark gray disturbance of the image runs through the circle, trembling. This, too, is a work that appropriates some historical piece: It is the blurred projection of Gil Wolman's early experimental film *L'Anti-Concept*. Seen in the constellation with *Dreamachine* it also establishes a reflexive convolution of inside and outside, subject and object: the aesthetic experience is not without object (it does not exist as a purely interior experience); the aesthetic object, in turn, becomes aesthetic only in and through the experience that occurs as a result of it (it does not exist "as such" in an exterior that is neutral with respect to the experience). At the same time, however, the constellation of the two projections, both reduced to the edge of the cinematic, points to two supplementary strands of experimental film of the 1960s and 1970s, namely, the reflection on cinematic means, on the one hand, and the various experiments with the psychedelic potential of film on the other. Both strands, however, aimed at liberating cinematic experience from a fixation on the story. The goal was to free the audience's mental activity from its being hold spellbound by filmic illusionism and, at least potentially, release its own productivity.

When, with his dual projections, Wyn Evans shatters in advance, as it were, the more or less solid bond between representation and represented in cinematic illusionism, the result is not a semantically empty positivity of representation but, as in his other installations, a process that is always stretched onto an open horizon of possible meanings. In Wyn Evan's version of *Dreamachine* such a horizon is introduced above all by means of a complex collage of sound: in addition to the legendary Master Musicians of Joujouka, the voice of Brion Gysin, and the recording of the Benny Golson classic *Whisper Not* by Art Blakey and His Jazz Messengers that Guy Debord used for the soundtrack of one of his last film critical films, it also includes Marcel Broodthaers discussing his work *Un jardin d'hiver*, of which the palms in the installation are a visual citation. In different ways the various historical recordings begin to communicate with what one sees, but the two never coincide completely. This also holds, mutatis mutandis, for the installation *The sky is thin as paper here...II* (the title is taken from a William S. Burroughs story): a photograph projected from Pierre Zucca and Pierre Klossowski's *La monnaie vivante* – it shows Klossowski's wife, Denise, in the sexually ambivalent role of the emancipated prostitute Roberte, who subjugates herself with an air of superiority, sitting on a man's lap – is also associated with a sound work. As in *Dreamachine* here too the acoustic material quotes important figures in the pre- and early history of installation art: excerpts from the music of Iannis Xenakis, John Cage, and Erik Satie (*Vexations*), which is no longer organized dynamically but spatially, are played for us as well as Broodthaer's voice again. Whereas the slide projection in *The sky is thin as paper here...II* is only indirectly revealed through the sound of the spatial aspect that was, of course, always latently present within it, in the case of *Dreamachine* not only the two projections but also the sound is from the outset part of a spatial arrangement that in turn, thanks in particular to the palms, so typical of Broodthaer's work, recall his interior installations. In both cases, however, the reference to one of the most important founding figures of installation art, Marcel Broodthaers, takes into account the circumstance that it is the art form of installation that continues to radicalize the antiobjectivist impulses of modern music and experimental film. Like both the latter, installation art is aimed against objectivist conceptions of aesthetic experience that reduce it to a synchronous coexecution of the temporal and dynamic progression of a piece of music or the dramatic plot of a film. Wyn Evans's recourse to the spatializing tendencies in music and the various strands of experimental film makes this historical connection explicit at the same time that his installations concentrate this motif into one semantic aspect of precisely the potentially endless experience that he is trying to liberate in the tradition of his aesthetic predecessors.

The same anti-objectivist development which lead the temporal arts (music, theater, film) to resist the idea of an experience that is synchronized with the work lead the spatial arts (painting, sculpture, photography) to oppose the idea that they could be comprehended instantly.

It was precisely this opposition that was, for Michael Fried, the true scandal of Minimal Art. Rather than persuading him at a glance, minimalist objects involved him in a process that is essentially unending; rather than a work that stood manifest at every moment, he found objects that opened up to the situation in which he found himself with them; in lieu of the work's objective impartiality there was an emphatic dependence on the performative perspective of the viewer.[05] Against Fried's objectivist and ultimately vestigially metaphysical conception of the artwork, however, it is possible, as I have already hinted above, to elucidate the structurally unending experience toward which minimalist objects entice us by means of their withdrawal as a genuinely aesthetic one. The fact that and the way in which minimalist objects, and today the installation art that follows in their wake, relate to the viewer does not derive from motives alien to art but, on the contrary, from a full claim to their aesthetic status. Thus it is no wonder that contemporary art returns again and again to historical Minimal Art and employs its logic in new ways. Liam Gillick's *Applied Resignation Platform*, a work created for the Frankfurter Kunstverein in 1999, should also be seen in this context. He replaced the opaque white plates of glass in the skylight of one of the upstairs rooms with colored Plexiglas. The installation, which alludes to, among other things, the surfaces in the work of Donald Judd, has remained in the Kunstverein on extended loan; whether it is exhibited, removed, or transformed is left up to subsequent artists. It is in keeping with the logic of Cerith Wyn Evans's respectful approach to historical, and here contemporary, predecessors that he picked up the ball and replaced Gillick's colored Plexiglass plates with transparent glass.

The result is integrated harmoniously with the exhibition. Not only do both the neon tubes visible behind the ceiling construction and the concrete structure of the ceiling itself recall the neon works shown on

---

[05] SEE FRIED, "ART AND OBJECTHOOD," (NOTE 2). ON THIS, SEE JULIANE REBENTISCH, *ÄSTHETIK DER INSTALLATION* (FRANKFURT AM MAIN: SUHRKAMP, 2003), ESP. 40–81.

the floor below – *Moebius Strip* and *Slow Fade to Black (Reversed)* – the work also literally sheds new light on the photographs by Wyn Evans's father, Sulwyn, that are presented in more or less traditional fashion in the same room and elsewhere in the building. They no longer seem like self-contained works but instead open up to the installation in which they have been introduced; they become a part of the large work that is formed by the Frankfurt exhibition as a whole through variously networking its individual elements. For example, the title that Wyn Evans gave his father's physiognomic studies in wood – *Anthropomorphic Portraits* – links it to the strange anthropomorphism of the chandeliers installed next door. Like in the case of the latter, the anthropomorphism of the portraits remains latent: it is impossible to say whether the wood is masking itself in anthropomorphic features that it does not really have or whether, conversely, it is concealing an anthropomorphic core beneath its material wooden surface. Our experience here oscillates between a literalness that has always been permeated with meaning and a meaning that is constantly withdrawing into the literal. In this way the biological father's photographs exhibited in the exhibition communicate with the works of the intellectual father figures who are cited in various ways in the exhibition. Like the latter, moreover, they can also be read as a reference to the artist's persona. In one of the photographs he even appears himself, as a child. Of course, this gesture of biographical self-staging cannot simply be filed away as a legend of the artist that is meant to explain the work. His father's photographs in the exhibition are countered by a wall text that casts doubt on the value of early photographs as documentary proof. The solar systems and galaxies identified in early astronomic photographs were often in truth nothing other than traces of dust particles or scales that had gotten into the photographic developer. The play of semblance and reality that Wyn Evans set in motion in his works by alluding to his private and professional life does not, of course, lie on this technical level. Nevertheless, despite the indexically clear relationships and historically clear connections, no conclusive evidence can be produced, the empirical existence of the person is never transparent through the semblance of the *mise en scène*. *Future Anterior* can also, perhaps, be understood as an emblem of an artistic self-staging that does not allow itself to be placed in the service of a depth hermeneutics of the artist´s intention: an orchid that is supposedly watered with a fluid containing phosphor, clichéd epitome of the artist as dandy, in whose empty depths, however, there is nothing but the projections of the viewer that keep approaching.

The sensibility of the dandy – "Masque ou décor, salut! J'adore ta beauté," Baudelaire wrote[06] – that is also evident elsewhere in the look of this quite elegant exhibition does not, however, inspire praise of the surface to be enjoyed as such but instead an experience that again and again throws viewers back on themselves and their projective powers. In and through the experience of the works viewers are confronted not least by themselves, for it is their own production of meaning that they encounter in the distorting mode of aesthetic semblance. *Inverse Reverse Perverse* is Wyn Evan's title for a large, concave mirrored object whose surface is based on the curvature of the lens of a human eye and whose radius corresponds to the dimensions of an average person as standardized by Le Corbusier. This object reflects the viewers moving around in the room, but right and left, top and bottom are reversed, the image of the viewer being moreover slightly distorted, especially as one gets closer to the object. It thus follows in the series of installations that since the mid-1970s have used the medium of art to reflect explicitly on the constitutive role that the viewer plays for the aesthetic status of artworks. The aesthetic intertwinement with the work, however, means that the viewers themselves are to some degree theatricalized, and this too becomes a theme in *Inverse Reverse Perverse*. Entering the process of

---

[06] CHARLES BAUDELAIRE, "TABLEAUX PARISIENS," IN IDEM, *LES FLEURS DU MAL/DIE BLUMEN DES BÖSEN* (STUTTGART: RECLAM, 1980), 206.

aesthetic experience means being surrounded and infected by the stage presence of the works – their indistinguishable double presence as thing and sign – and to be placed on stage oneself: to become an actor who plays out the tense relation of the two poles of the work's double presence performatively. Precisely because the relationship to the work is essentially indeterminate, and finds secure footing neither in a symbolic meaning nor in the positivity of the form, viewers will reflect on their own part, their role in this relationship, on that which they – each for her- or himself – do in this situation. The aesthetic experience is thus realized in a reflective interruption of our usual access to things, in an act of distancing oneself from the self-evidence of our cultural and social background assumptions that *perverts*, if you will, the normality of our being-in-the-world. Precisely in this reflective distance that is established by aesthetically experienced objects, in a distance that bars any immediate understanding as well as any merely sybaritic and consumerist approach, there is also, I believe, a moment of resistance of art to the commodity, of the image to the visual, of the theater to the spectacle.

As if to remain faithful with this potential of the aesthetic to the project of the critics of the spectacle and the culture industry, Debord and Adorno, they stand at the center of the works that open and close the exhibition in the foyer of the Kunstverein. At the stairs going to the upper floor Wyn Evans has placed a red neon sign that forms a closed circle and quotes the Latin palindrome that Guy Debord chose as the title of one of his last films: *In girum imus nocte et consumimur igni* (We walk at night in a circle and are consumed by flame). To its side a plain modern lamp blinks Adorno's message in a bottle in Morse code.

TRANSLATED FROM THE GERMAN BY STEVEN LINDBERG.

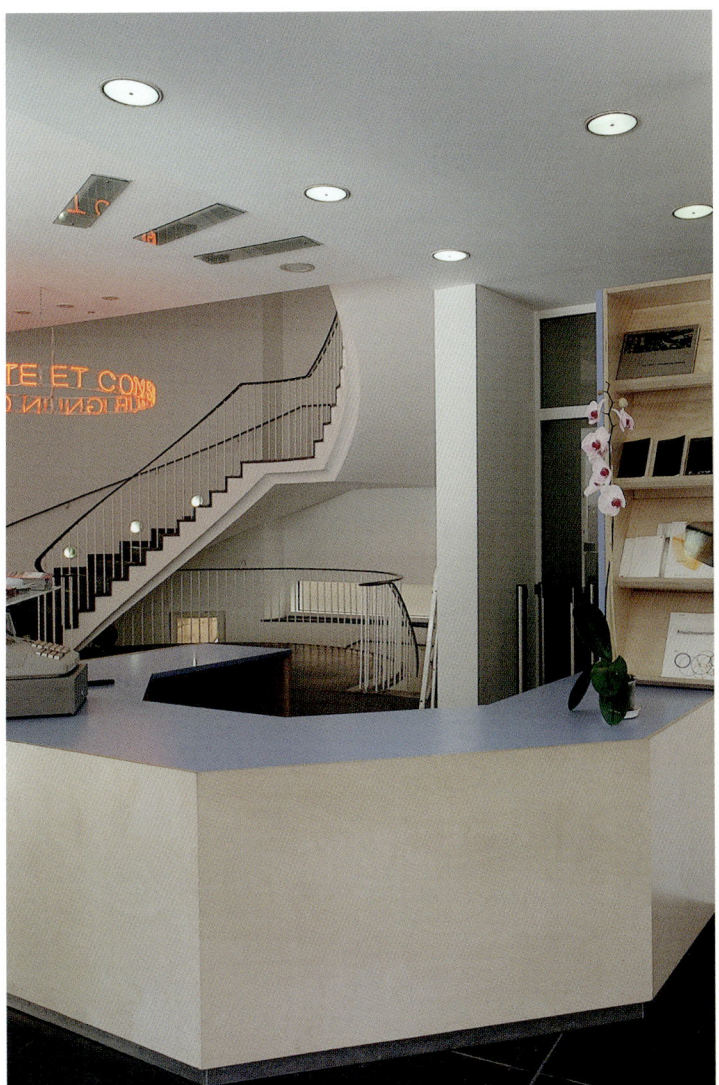

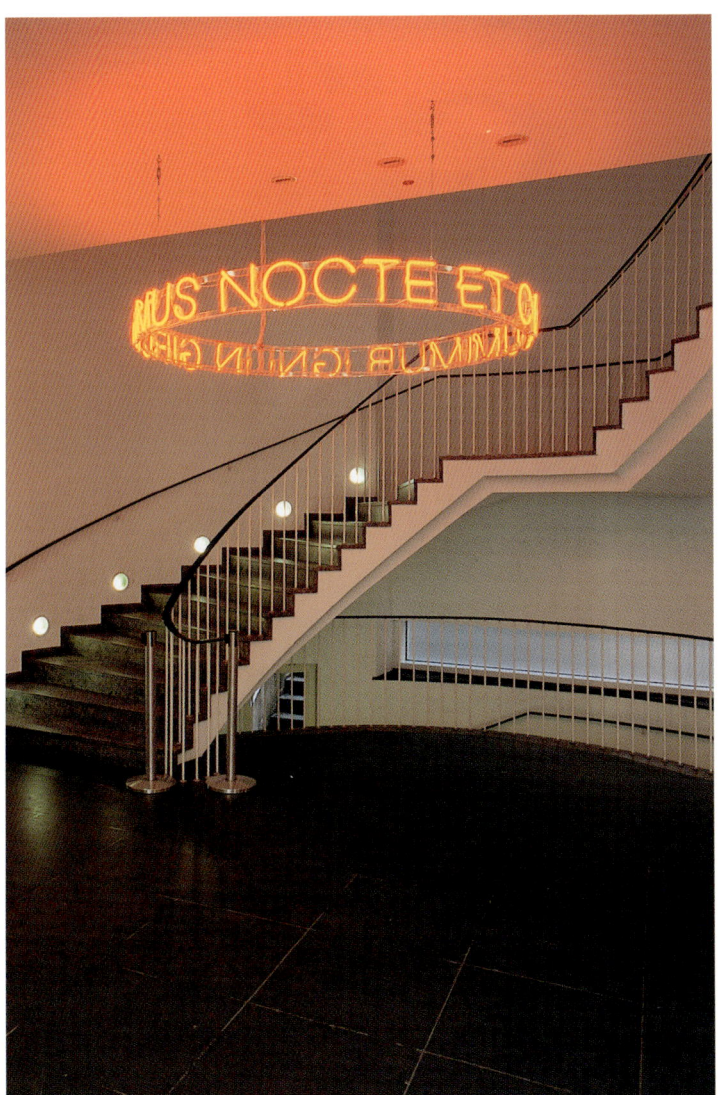

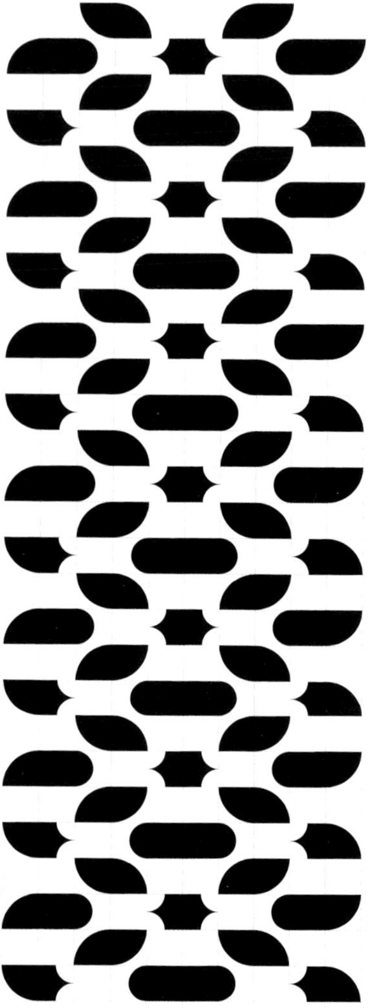

Dreama-
chine Plan
(45 RPM)

Instructions

- Paperclip or lightly glue this plan over a large piece of card.
- Cut through the plan and card around the perimeter of the black shapes.
- Remove the plan and connect the ends of the card together to form a cylinder (make sure the holes on either side of the joint are at the same spacing as the others on the Dreamachine). It may be necessary to score the card slightly so that it remains round.
- Place the cylinder on the centre of a record turntable, set the speed to 45 rpm.
- Suspend a light source in the centre of the cylinder. A cantilevered arm will serve adequately to overreach the centre of the cylinder and a normal lighting socket with bulb can be suspended from this. The light should be roughly one third to halfway down the cylinder (experiment to see which one you find best.) Care should be taken to ensure the light does not touch the cylinder or turntable when in use.
- Sit comfortably (and well balanced) with your face close to the centre of the columns.
- View the Dreamachine with your eyes closed. A kaleidoscope of light will result and slowly these will turn into archetypal visions.

Warning: The Dreamachine may be hazardous to people with epilepsy or other nervous disorders. Please use with caution.

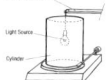

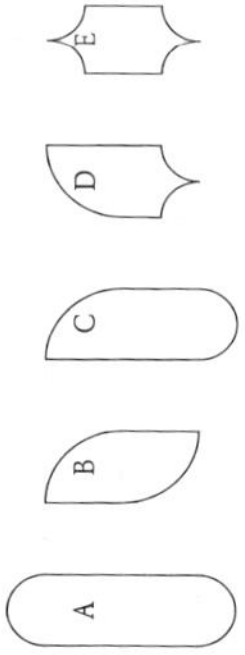

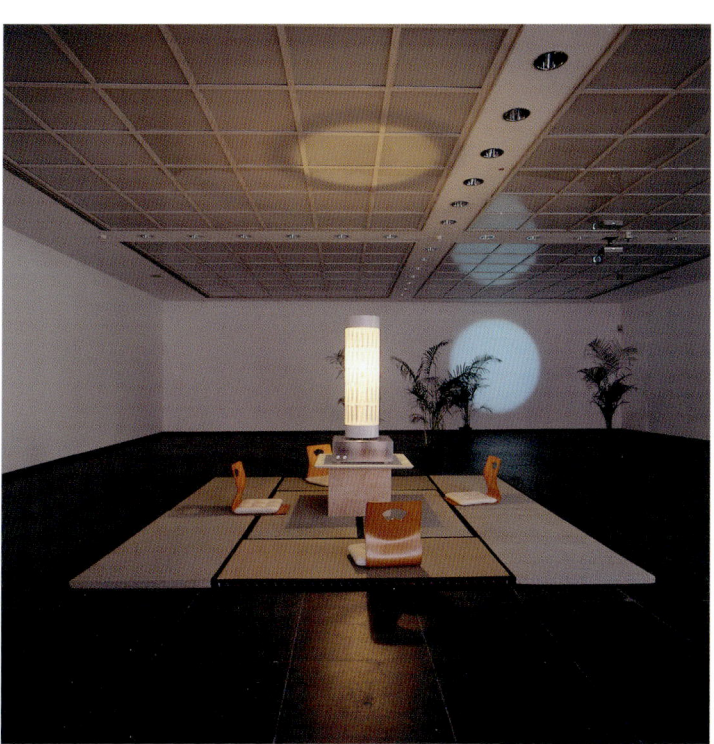

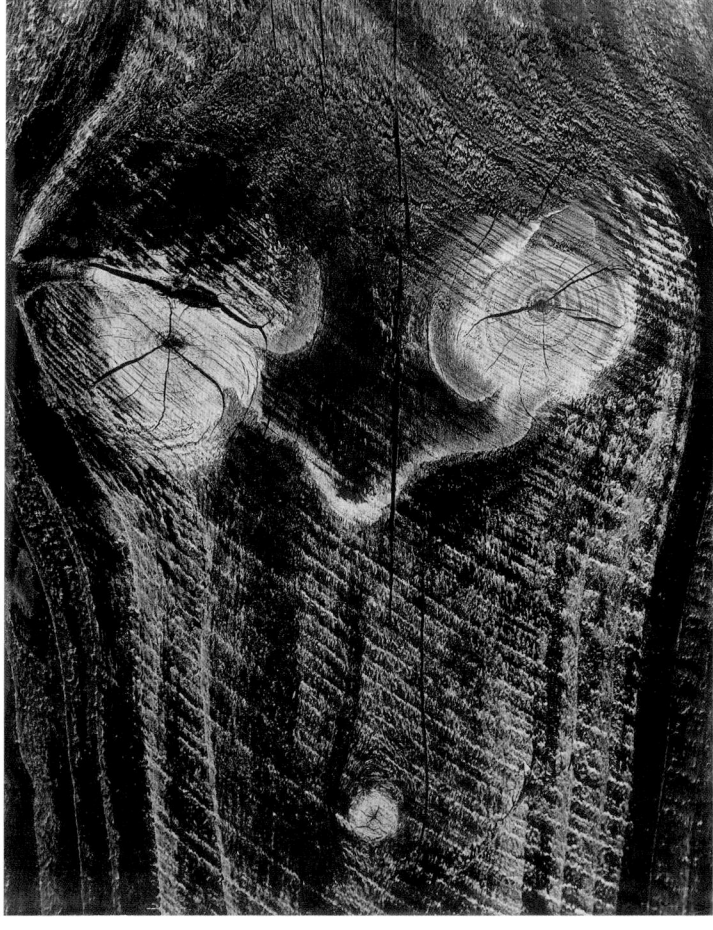

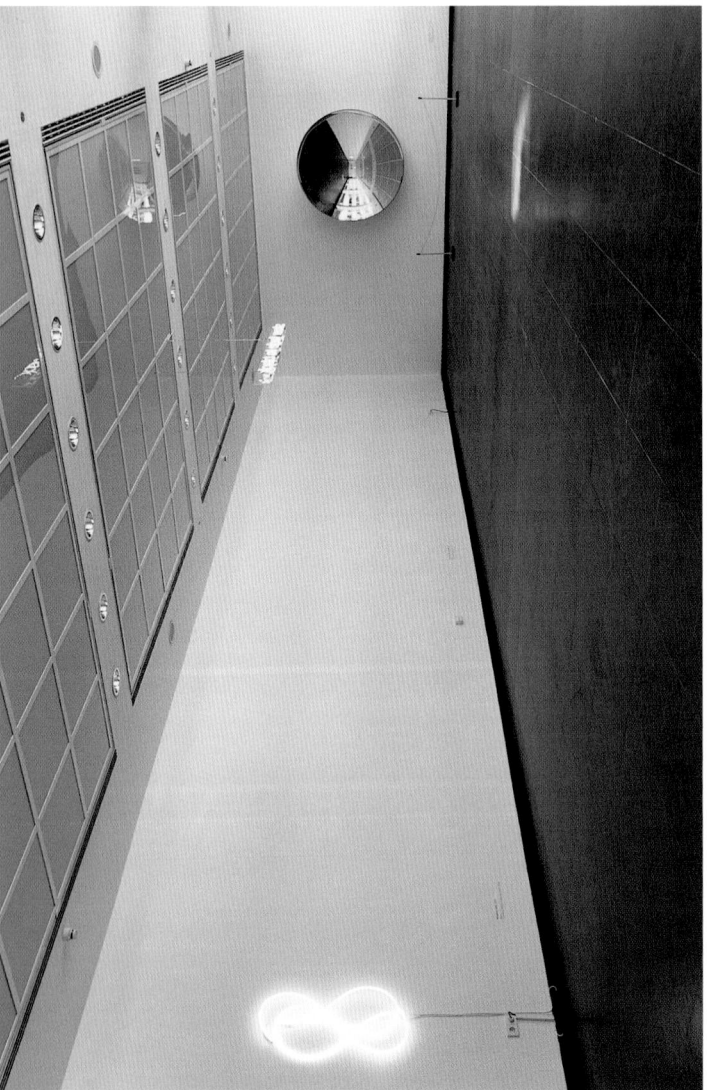

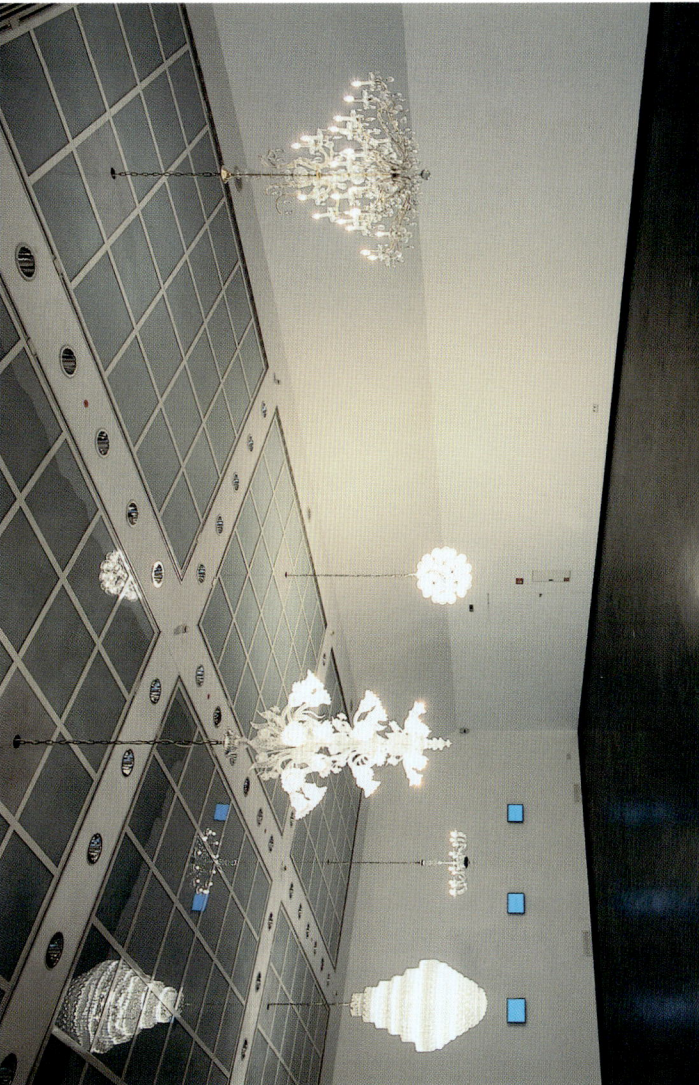

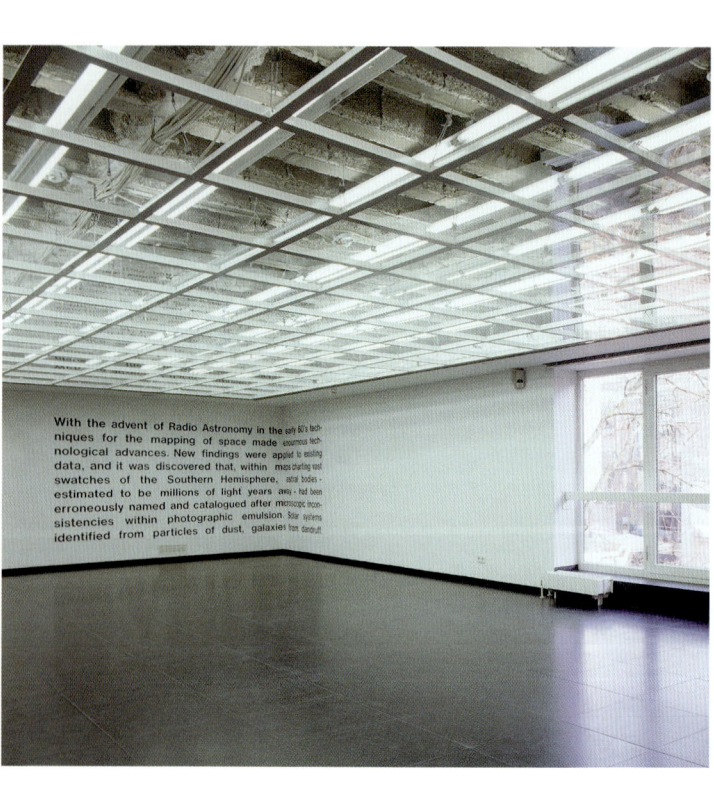

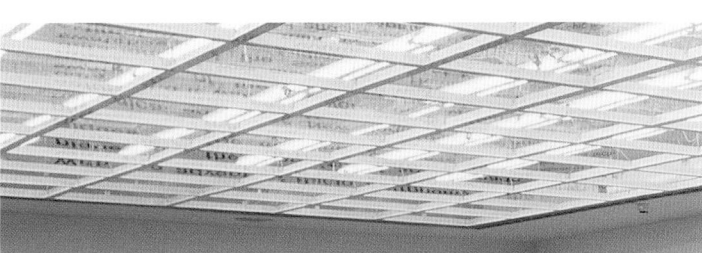

With the advent of Radio Astronomy in the early 60's techniques for the mapping of space made enourmous technological advances. New findings were applied to existing data, and it was discovered that, within maps charting vast swatches of the Southern Hemisphere, astral bodies - estimated to be millions of light years away - had been erroneously named and catalogued after microscopic inconsistencies within photographic emulsion. Solar systems identified from particles of dust, galaxies from dandruff.

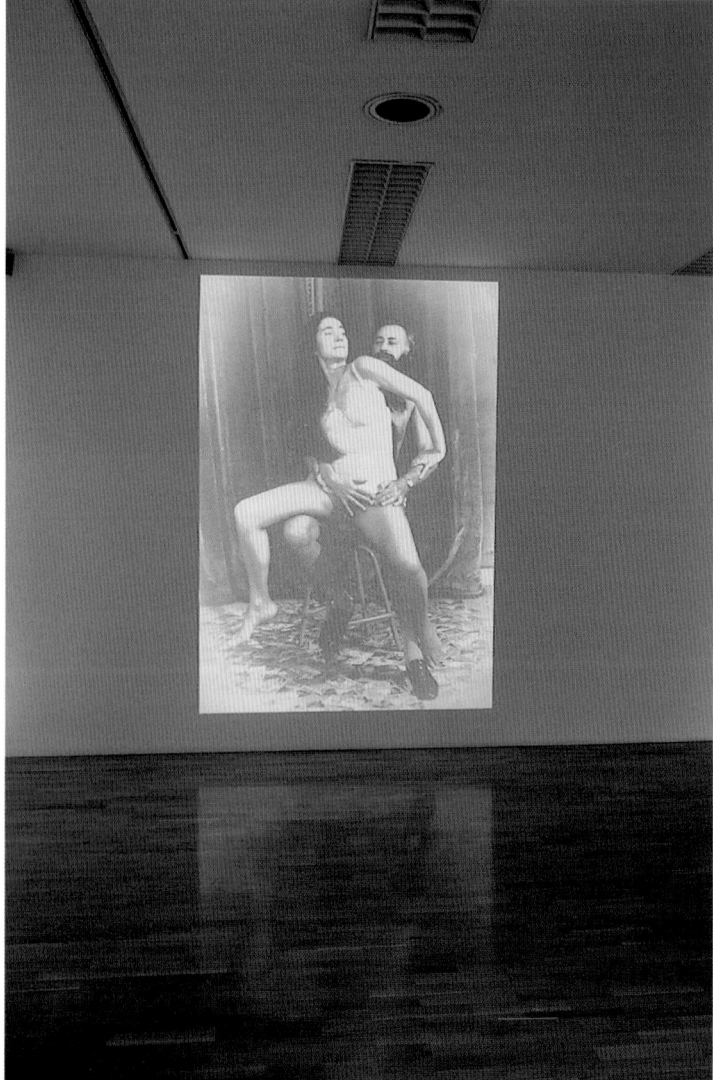

Future Anterior, 1994
Phaleonopsis Orchid treated with phosphorus liquid
Dimsensions variable

In Girum Imus Nocte Et Consumimur Igni, 1998
Neon
Diametre 176 cm, hight: 20 cm
EVN Collection, Vienna

Dreamachine, 1998
Mixed media, Japanese seatings, tatami mats, plants
Dimensions variable

Dreamachine Plan (45 RPM)
Flickers of the Dreamachine, ed. by Paul Cecil, The Book Factory, London 1996

Face in Wood Grain 1, 2003
Photograph by Sulwyn Evans, 51,1 x 40,3 cm
Private collection, Cologne

Installation view Frankfurter Kunstverein

„*Look at that picture...How does it appear to you now? Does it seem to be persisting?*", 2003
Mixed media
Dimensions variable

Applied Resignation Platform by Liam Gillick, 1999, *modified*, 2004, *by Cerith Wyn Evans*

Text accompanying photographs
Installation view Frankfurter Kunstverein

The sky is thin as paper here ...II, 2004
Slide projection

JULIANE REBENTISCH
DAS ENTKOLONISIERTE THEATER

IM THEATRALISCHEN UNLESBAREN, IN DER NACHT, DIE DEM BUCH VORAUSGEHT, IST DAS ZEICHEN NOCH NICHT VON DER KRAFT GESCHIEDEN. ES IST NOCH NICHT GANZ ZEICHEN, IN DEM SINNE, WIE WIR ES VERSTEHEN, ES IST ABER AUCH KEIN *DING* MEHR, DAS WIR NUR IM GEGENSATZ ZUM ZEICHEN DENKEN KÖNNEN. ES HAT DAHER KEINE MÖGLICHKEIT MEHR, ALS SOLCHES GESCHRIEBENER TEXT ODER ARTIKULIERTE REDE ZU WERDEN: KEINE MÖGLICHKEIT MEHR, SICH ÜBER DIE *ENERGEIA* ZU ERHEBEN UND SICH AUFZUBLÄHEN, UM SICH ... IN DIE DÜSTERE UND OBJEKTIVE UNPARTEILICHKEIT DES *ERGON* ZU KLEIDEN.[01] (JACQUES DERRIDA)

Opening Night im Frankfurter Kunstverein: unten Soziales, lose gruppiert um die Figur des Künstlers; oben jeder allein gelassen mit den Szenen, die er dort „für uns", sein Publikum, inszeniert hat, um in ihnen jedoch sogleich jede mögliche Kollektivität aufzulösen. Wollte man hinsichtlich der installativen Arrangements von Cerith Wyn Evans von Theater sprechen, so wäre dies ein Theater, das man nur alleine besuchen kann, ein Theater, das sich nicht im Dabeisein erschließt, sondern das den Einzelnen erwartet, um sich ereignen zu können. Es zieht sich denn auch kein Vorhang zurück; alles ist schon da, wenn man eintritt, und alles bleibt dort, wenn man die Szenen in einem Moment gewaltsamer Willkür wieder verlässt. Denn was sich dazwischen ereignet, hat keine messbare Aufführungs- oder Vorführzeit, an die sich die Erfahrung halten könnte; es gibt hier kein objektives Ende, nach dem man sich beruhigt mit einem lässig selbstgewissen „Done that" abwenden könnte. Und es gibt auch kein dramatisches Geschehen, das unsere Aufmerksamkeit entlang der Linien einer Geschichte oder eines allegorischen Sinns zum Ziel einer Erkenntnis leiten könnte. Dennoch gibt es hier etwas wie Theater.

Ein Theater der Zeichen und der Dinge zum Beispiel, wie in einem der oberen Ausstellungsräume, dessen ansonsten recht neutrale Atmosphäre sich nun mit der Melancholie eines verlassenen, allein von den Requisiten vergangener Welten belebten Ballsaals überlagert. Bereits

---

[01] JACQUES DERRIDA: „DIE SOUFFLIERTE REDE". IN: DERS.: *DIE SCHRIFT UND DIE DIFFERENZ*, FRANKFURT AM MAIN 1972. S. 259–301. HIER: S. 292.

die Belebung des Raums durch die Dinge hat eine deutlich theatralische Qualität, denn sie ist hier ganz wörtlich zu nehmen: Fünf verschiedene Kronleuchter besetzen in ihrer je individuellen Opulenz souverän den Raum; ihr ungleichzeitig an- und ausgehendes Licht sendet Signale, Morse-Signale, wie sich bald herausstellt. Jeder Leuchter überträgt dabei einen anderen Text. An den diskret an der Wand installierten Flachbildschirmen erscheinen die Texte in der Geschwindigkeit ihrer Übersetzung – oder Aufführung – durch das beeindruckende Lichtspiel, das uns mit seiner stummen Polyphonie aus Hell und Dunkel im Rücken liegt, wenn wir die Texte im gleichbleibend bläulichen Licht der Monitore zu lesen beginnen. Als versuchten wir, während einer Theateraufführung mittels eines Programmheftes die Schauspieler ihren Rollen zuzuordnen, suchen wir nun die Kronleuchter mit den Texten zu identifizieren. Was für eine Konstellation! Ein klassisch eleganter Barovier & Torso-Leuchter „spricht" ein Stück Text aus einem Interviewband mit dem Künstler, Schriftsteller und Burroughs-Mitstreiter Brion Gysin, in dem dieser von seiner Begegnung mit dem professionellen Medium Eileen Garrett erzählt; ein moderner, kompakt runder Leuchter von Achille Castiglione überträgt einen Ausschnitt aus dem vermutlich von mehreren Personen aus dem Salon der Madame de Lafayette verfassten Roman *La Princesse de Clèves*, dem ersten literarischen Dokument des Konzepts romantischer Liebe; Auszüge aus den gesammelten Schriften von John Cage werden durch ein enorm ausladendes, eher an ein Feuerwerk denn noch an eine Lampe gemahnendes Objekt von Venini Quadratti aufgeführt; ein mit floralen Motiven spielendes, längliches Modell von Galliano Ferro übersetzt Überlegungen der Literaturwissenschaftlerin und Queer-Studies-Theoretikerin Eve Kosofsky Sedgwick zur tendenziell paranoiden Struktur einer Leseerfahrung, bei der sich die Position des Lesers im Text selber zu reflektieren scheint; und schließlich sendet uns ein antiker Kronleuchter ein kleines Stück aus Theodor W. Adornos „The Stars Down to Earth", einer sozialpsychologischen Studie über eine Astrologie-Kolumne der *Los Angeles Times*.

Tatsächlich werden die fünf Leuchter in dieser Anordnung potenziell zu Darstellern, nicht nur der sehr verschiedenen Texte, sondern auch von deren AutorInnen. Momentweise, besonders in den Augenblicken des Nachglühens der Birnen im Halbdunkel, nehmen sie eine geradezu anthropomorphe Qualität an; werden zu Medien weniger im kommunikationstechnischen denn im okkulten Sinne. Dennoch geht die leise unheimliche Wirkung ihres Schauspiels nicht in den Bezügen auf, die sich auf der semantischen Ebene zwischen der frühen Medientheorie und den parapsychologischen Fähigkeiten der glamourösen Eileen Garrett herstellen lassen. Vielmehr besteht sie grundsätzlicher noch in der *Latenz* solch anthropomorpher Qualitäten unterhalb der manifesten Dingqualität der Leuchter. Sie besteht mit anderen Worten darin, dass diese – wie auch immer luxuriösen – Gebrauchsdinge überhaupt quasi-subjektive Züge annehmen können. Denn genau dies wird ja nie offen vorgeführt. Eben in einem solchermaßen *maskierten* Anthropomorphismus hatte Michael Fried 1967 in einem später berühmt gewordenen Text über die provozierend einfachen Objekte der Minimal Art einen entscheidenden Aspekt dessen gesehen, was er in kritischer Absicht deren „Theatralität" nannte.[02] Was die schlichten Objekte der Minimal Art in dieser Hinsicht mit den alles andere als schlichten Kronleuchtern teilen, die Cerith Wyn Evans für seine Inszenierung gecastet hat, ist ihre theatrale Doppelpräsenz: Ein Stuhl auf der Bühne ist immer zugleich ein einfacher Stuhl und Zeichen für etwas anderes, den Thron von King Lear beispielsweise; ein Schauspieler auf der Bühne zeigt immer zugleich sich selbst und etwas anderes, den dramatischen Charakter. Im Unterschied aber zum traditionellen dramatischen Theater, wo Schauspieler und Bühnenrequisiten möglichst auf die von ihnen dargestellte dramatische Welt transparent werden sollen, die Ebene der Darstellung hinter das Dargestellte zurücktreten soll, bleibt das theatrale Spannungsverhältnis zwischen

---

[02] MICHAEL FRIED: „KUNST UND OBJEKTHAFTIGKEIT", IN: *MINIMAL ART. EINE KRITISCHE RETROSPEKTIVE*, HRSG. VON GREGOR STEMMRICH, DRESDEN/BASEL 1995, S. 334-374. VGL. BES. S. 345 FF.

Darstellendem und Dargestelltem im Falle der Kronleuchter-Installation dezidiert unaufgelöst.

Wir haben es hier mit einer Inszenierung ohne eigentliches Drama zu tun, mit einem von der Herrschaft des Dramas gleichsam entkolonisierten Theater. Zwar gibt es auch hier Text, aber dieser tritt buchstäblich *neben* die anderen Darstellungsmittel – und damit selbst als eines hervor. Zeichen für Zeichen erscheint die Schrift langsam auf den Monitoren und verselbständigt sich so partiell gegenüber dem von ihr Bedeuteten. Zudem unterhält der Text ein eher abstraktes Verhältnis zu den Lichtsignalen, die ihn codieren; diese nämlich sind für uns trotz der Suggestion ihrer Lesbarkeit zunächst einmal unlesbar. Das Darstellende wird hier nicht auf ein Dargestelltes hin durchsichtig, vielmehr treten Darstellendes und Dargestelltes in ein Spannungsverhältnis, das sich an keinem der Pole, weder bei der dinglichen oder medientechnischen Faktizität der Leuchter noch aber bei einem bestimmten Textsinn auflösen lässt. Beide Pole sind uns nur im widerstreitenden Bezug aufeinander gegeben. Dadurch, dass die Leuchter der unauffälligen Vertrautheit ihres gewöhnlichen Gebrauchskontextes entrückt sind, kommt zwar ihre elektrisch-gläserne Medialität als solche in den Blick; doch tritt uns diese hier eben nicht positivistisch als bloßes Sinnesdatum entgegen, sondern in und durch ihren gespannten Bezug auf einen offenen Horizont möglicher Bedeutungen. Gespannt ist dieser Bezug, weil die Sinndimensionen, die das intertextuelle Gewebe zwischen Gysin, Madame de Lafayette, Cage, Sedgwick und Adorno hervorbringen mag, sich nie an den Leuchtern objektiv dingfest machen lassen, sondern nur – momentweise, ähnlich den kurzen Intervallen eines Morsesignals – an ihnen aufscheinen, um sich im nächsten Augenblick wieder unverbindlich in das zu neuen Bedeutungsbildungen anreizende Lichtspiel der blinkenden Oberflächen zurückzustellen.

Die Bühnenpräsenz dieser Leuchter besteht mithin nicht darin, dass sie ein bestimmtes Etwas (einen Text, eine Person, einen medien-, literatur-, kunst- oder gesellschaftstheoretischen Sinn) verkörpern oder symbolisieren, sondern darin, dass sie uns, je einzeln, in einen Prozess verwickeln, in dem sich unsere Sinnproduktion letztlich immer notwendig als Sinnprojektion erweisen muss, um sich dann nur wieder erneut an ihrem Deutungspotenzial zu entzünden. In der Tat sind wir hier *im* Werk (Sedgwick[03]); es ist allein *für uns* – allein im Prozess unserer letztlich unbeendbaren Verstehensvollzüge wird das Werk ins Werk gesetzt: als Kunstwerk frei. Die Bühnenpräsenz der Leuchter, ihre ästhetische Qualität, entfaltet sich in einer wesentlich individuellen Erfahrung, die das Spannungsverhältnis zwischen Ding und Zeichen prozessual austrägt. Was sich hier am Werk ereignet, spielt in jenem nächtlichen Bereich des Nicht-mehr und Noch-nicht (Derrida), der sich den an betrachter- und kontextunabhängiger Objektivität orientierten Kategorien der modernistischen Werkästhetik offenbar entzieht. Der Prozess, in den wir hier, in dieser Installation, eintreten, lässt sich weder objektivistisch an den in ihr versammelten Texten oder Gegenständen festmachen noch aber subjektivistisch allein der imaginativen Leistung der BetrachterInnen zurechnen. *Look at that picture...*, so Evans im Titel seiner Installation, *How does it appear to you now? Does it seem to be persisting?* Die Bedeutungen, die auf die eine oder andere Weise an seinem Werk *erscheinen*, sind dort weder einfach objektiv vorzufinden noch aber sind sie von uns intentional hineingelesen worden. Wir erfahren uns hier als performativ, als hervorbringend, ohne jedoch die entsprechend wirkenden Kräfte gänzlich unter unsere Kontrolle bringen zu können.

Was sich aber aus der objektivistischen Perspektive der modernistischen Werkästhetik, wie sie etwa von dem Theatralitätskritiker Michael Fried vertreten wird, nur als Kontrollverlust und Entfremdung (vom Objekt ebenso wie vom Selbst) beschreiben lässt, könnte man im kritischen Anschluss an die kantische Tradition auch Lust nennen: die

---

[03] EVE KOSOFSKY SEDGWICK: „PARANOID READING AND REPARATIVE READING, OR, YOU'RE SO PARANOID, YOU PROBABLY THINK THIS ESSAY IS ABOUT YOU", IN: DIES.: *TOUCHING FEELING: AFFECT, PEDAGOGY, PERFORMATIVITY*. DURHAM/LONDON 2003.

selbstreflexive Erfahrung der Entfaltung subjektiver Kräfte in und durch den Bezug auf einen ästhetischen Gegenstand. Auf der Seite des Objekts spiegelt sich diese Erfahrung im Begriff des ästhetischen Scheins. Denn Schein kann in der nachkantischen Tradition der philosophischen Ästhetik jenes „selbständig gewordene Unselbständige" heißen, als das man die ästhetische Erfahrung in ihrem Leisten, ihrer Performanz begreifen muss.[04] Die Performativität der ästhetischen Erfahrung wäre dann allerdings nicht im Sinne eines Handlungsvollzugs, sondern im Sinne eines Ereignisses *zwischen* Subjekt und Objekt zu verstehen, das dem erfahrenden Subjekt eher widerfährt denn intentional von ihm vollzogen wird. Es ist dies eine Erfahrung, die sich unmittelbar weder in Erkenntnis noch in Handlung übersetzen lässt, eine Erfahrung mithin, die aufgrund ihrer Eigenlogik – der Eigenlogik des Ästhetischen – einen autonomen Bereich neben den Sphären der theoretischen und der praktischen Vernunft einnimmt. In diesem Sinne bringt gerade die theatralische Kunst in der Nachfolge der Minimal Art reflexiv Grundzüge jeder eigentlich ästhetischen Erfahrung heraus, die von der modernistischen Werkästhetik zuvor marginalisiert wurden: deren selbstreflexiv-performative Qualität ebenso wie deren prinzipielle Unendlichkeit.

In Frankfurt findet die verflochtene Korrespondenz zwischen Werk und Betrachter, bei der sich ein bestimmter Sinnzusammenhang im einen Augenblick ins Zentrum ästhetischer Signifikanz falten mag, um sich im nächsten als bloß äußerliche Projektion aus diesem wieder zurückzuziehen und damit potenziell endlos Raum für Neues zu geben, ein gleichsam theoretisches Bild in der Ausstellung selbst: In einem anderen Raum hängt in der Form verschlungener Neonröhren die stilisierte Darstellung des berühmten Möbiusbandes (*Moebius Strip*, 1997), das bekanntermaßen so verdreht ist, dass man von seiner Außenseite auf die Innenseite und umgekehrt gleiten kann, ohne jemals den Rand zu überschreiten. Aber auch eine solche metaästhetische

---

[04] RÜDIGER BUBNER: *ÄSTHETISCHE ERFAHRUNG*, FRANKFURT AM MAIN 1989, S. 39.

Lesart ist natürlich nichts als eine Projektion, *Schein*. Wiederum wird dessen nächtliche Arbeit hier aber nicht zugunsten einer vermeintlichen Objektivität des „eigentlichen Werks" dementiert, sondern gleichsam räumlich reflektiert. Neben *Slow fade to black (reversed)*, einem Neonschriftzug, der spiegelverkehrt so an der Decke installiert wurde, dass er sich in der gegenüberliegenden Fensterscheibe lesen lässt, erscheint auch der sich im selben Fenster spiegelnde Abglanz des *Moebius Strips* momentweise als das eigentliche Zentrum des Werks; und das brutalistische Gebäude, auf das der Kunstverein ausblickt, als Teil der Arbeit. Im Falle von *Slow fade to black (reversed)* erhält die Inszenierung des Außen im Innen und des Innen im Außen, das reversible Gleiten der Bedeutungen auf dem Rand zwischen beidem, eine deutlich filmische Qualität. Die durch das Fenster im Cinemascope-Format gerahmte Betonarchitektur erscheint wie ein Filmbild; der Neon-Schriftzug wie ein brechtianisch die filmischen Verfahren ausstellender Untertitel, der ankündigt, dass sich das Bild in wenigen Augenblicken in Schwärze aufgelöst haben wird. Das wird freilich nie eingelöst; das Schlussbild bleibt in der eigentümlichen Schwebe kurz vor seiner Auflösung hängen und verwandelt sich in eine Art „Duration Piece", das den kleinen Veränderungen der Lichtverhältnisse im Außenraum schleichend die Spannung von Hitchcocks *Rear Window* unterschiebt. Wie dem Theater so entziehen Wyn Evans´ Verfahren aber auch dem Film, der aufgrund seines größeren illusionistischen Potenzials heute in vielerlei Hinsicht die Funktionen des traditionellen dramatischen Theaters übernommen hat, dezidiert den Plot. Hier gibt es offensichtlich weder ein dramatisches Geschehen oder eine Story noch auch überhaupt eine Filmprojektion, nur die beiläufige Spiegelung eines Neonschriftzugs im Fenster. Wenn es hier dennoch Projektion gibt, so allein diejenige des Betrachters, der sich reflexiv in den unendlich Außen und Innen zusammenschließenden semantischen Schlaufen verfängt, die sich zwischen ihm und der Arbeit entspinnen.

In anderer Weise isoliert Wyn Evans die performativ-projektive Aktivität des Betrachters in einer weiteren, im weitesten Sinne filmischen

Installation, der *Dreamachine*. Inmitten eines von Palmen umgebenen japanischen Sitzinterieurs dreht sich auf einem minimalistischen Sockel ein zylinderförmiger, von Löchern durchsetzter Lampenschirm, der flottierende Lichtpunkte in den ansonsten eher dunklen Raum wirft. Richtet man seine geschlossenen Augen direkt auf die Lichtmaschine, so erscheinen auf der Netzhaut dynamische blassbunte Punkte, Muster gar. Die auf einen Entwurf von Brion Gysin und Ian Sommerville aus den sechziger Jahren zurückgehende *Dreamachine* verwirklicht damit auf eine sehr direkte, geradezu buchstäbliche Weise die Idee einer Art „Kino im Kopf", dessen imaginative Energien das Expanded Cinema jener Zeit gegen die intellektuelle Passivität mobilisieren wollte, zu welcher der immersive Illusionismus der kommerziellen Traumfabrik sein Publikum verdammt. Man muß nicht wissen, dass Wyn Evans vom Experimentalfilm kommt, um zu sehen, dass er diesem kritischen Projekt verpflichtet geblieben ist. In mehrfacher Weise wird es hier fortgesetzt. So wird den Lichtpunkten, welche die *Dreamachine* vor unser inneres Auge stellt, ein diese Erfahrung gleichsam externalisierendes Pendant zur Seite gestellt. Ein an der Decke montierter Beamer setzt einen Lichtkegel an die Wand, in dessen runder Weiße nichts als hellbunte Punkte zu sehen sind; ab und zu durchzieht zitternd, als eigentlich „filmischer" Effekt, eine schwarzgräuliche Bildstörung den Kreis. Auch dies ist wiederum eine Arbeit mit einer historischen Arbeit: Es handelt sich um die unscharfe Projektion von Gil Wolmans frühem Experimentalfilm *L´Anti-Concept*. In der Konstellation mit der *Dreamachine* ergibt sich zunächst wieder eine reflexive Verschlingung von Innen und Außen, Subjekt und Objekt: die ästhetische Erfahrung ist nicht ohne Gegenstand (es gibt sie nicht als rein innere); der ästhetische Gegenstand wiederum wird zum ästhetischen Gegenstand erst durch die Erfahrung, die sich an ihm vollzieht (es gibt ihn nicht „an sich" in einem gegenüber der Erfahrung neutralen Außen). Zugleich aber verweist die Gegenüberstellung der beiden bis an die Grenze des Filmischen reduzierten Projektionen auf zwei einander ergänzende Stränge des Experimentalfilms der sechziger und siebziger Jahre, nämlich auf die Reflexion der filmischen Mittel einerseits und auf die verschiedenen Experimente mit deren psychedelischem Potenzial andererseits. Beide Stränge zielten indes auf die Befreiung der Filmerfahrung von der Fixierung auf die Story. Die Bewusstseinstätigkeit des Publikums sollte aus ihrem illusionistischen Bann freigesetzt und, zumindest der Möglichkeit nach, in eine produktive Eigenlogik entlassen werden.

Wenn Wyn Evans mit seinen zwei Projektionen gleichsam vorab die im filmischen Illusionismus relativ fest gefügten Bande zwischen Darstellung und Dargestelltem durchschlägt, so geschieht dies nicht zugunsten einer semantisch leeren Positivität der Darstellung, sondern wiederum, wie auch in seinen anderen Installationen, zugunsten eines Prozesses, der stets auf einen offenen Horizont möglicher Bedeutungen gespannt bleibt. In Wyn Evans´ Version der *Dreamachine* wird ein solcher vor allem durch eine komplexe Soundcollage eingezogen: neben dem legendären Ensemble der Master Musicians of Joujouka, der Stimme von Brion Gysin und der Einspielung des Benny-Golson-Klassikers *Whisper Not* durch Art Blakey and his Jazz Messengers, die Guy Debord für den Soundtrack eines seiner letzten filmkritischen Filme verwendet hat, hört man unter anderem auch Marcel Broodthaers im Gespräch über seine Arbeit *Un jardin d´hiver*, die in der Installation durch die Palmen visuell zitiert wird. Auf unterschiedliche Weise beginnen die diversen historischen Aufnahmen mit dem Gesehenen zu kommunizieren, ohne doch je mit diesem vollständig zur Deckung zu kommen. Dies gilt in ähnlicher Weise auch für die nach einer Erzählung von William Burroughs betitelte Installation *The sky is thin as paper here…II*: Einem an die Wand projizierten Foto aus Pierre Zuccas und Pierre Klossowskis Buch *Lebendes Geld* – es zeigt Klossowskis Frau Denise in der sexuell ambivalenten Rolle der überlegen sich unterwerfenden, der emanzipiert sich prostituierenden Roberte auf dem Schoß eines Mannes – assoziiert sich dort ebenfalls eine Soundarbeit. Wie in der *Dreamachine* zitiert das akustische Material auch hier nicht zuletzt wichtige Figuren aus der modernen

Vor- und Frühgeschichte installativer Kunst: Ausschnitte aus der nicht mehr zeitlich-dynamisch, sondern gleichsam räumlich organisierten Musik von Iannis Xenakis, John Cage und Erik Satie (*Vexations*) werden uns ebenso zugespielt wie erneut die Stimme Broodthaers´. Während die Diaprojektion in *The sky is thin as paper here…II* erst indirekt durch den Sound in ihrem latent natürlich immer schon vorhandenen räumlichen Aspekt erschlossen wird, sind sowohl die beiden Projektionen als auch der Sound im Falle der *Dreamachine* von vornherein Teil eines räumlichen Arrangements, das als solches, vor allem durch die für Broodthaers typischen Palmen, an dessen installative Interieurs erinnert. In beiden Fällen aber mag der Bezug auf einen der wichtigsten Gründungsväter installativer Kunst, Marcel Broodthaers, dem Umstand Rechnung tragen, dass es die Kunstform der Installation ist, welche die antiobjektivistischen Impulse in der modernen Musik und im Experimentalfilm weiterführend radikalisiert. Wie diese richtet die Kunst der Installation sich nämlich gegen eine Idee der ästhetischen Erfahrung, die diese objektivistisch auf einen – sei´s mit dem zeitlich-dynamischen Verlauf des Musikstücks, sei´s mit dem dramatischen Geschehen des Films – synchronen Mitvollzug reduziert. Wyn Evans´ Rekurs auf die Verräumlichungstendenzen in der Musik und die verschiedenen Stränge des Experimentalfilms macht diesen historischen Zusammenhang im gleichen Zug explizit wie er ihn im Medium seiner Installationen auf ein Moment eben jener potenziell unendlichen Erfahrung verdichtet, die freizusetzen er in der Linie seiner ästhetischen Vorläufer angetreten ist.

Was für die Zeitkünste – Musik, Theater, Film – der Widerstand gegen die Idee einer mit dem Werk synchronen Erfahrung ist, ist für die Raumkünste – Malerei, Skulptur, Fotografie – die Opposition gegen die Idee von dessen augenblicklicher Erfassbarkeit. Eben dies – diese Opposition – war denn auch für Michael Fried der eigentliche Skandal der prä-installativen Minimal Art. Statt ihn mit einem Blick zu überzeugen, involvierten ihn die minimalistischen Objekte in einen Prozess, der wesentlich unbeendbar ist; statt eines in jedem Augenblick manifest in sich stehenden Werks fand er hier Objekte vor, die sich auf die Situation, in der er sich mit ihnen befand, entgrenzten; an die Stelle einer objektiven Unparteilichkeit des Werks trat dessen herausgestellte Abhängigkeit von der performativen Perspektive des Betrachters.[05] Gegen Frieds objektivistische und letztlich restmetaphysische Konzeption des Kunstwerks lässt sich indes, ich habe es oben bereits angedeutet, gerade die strukturell unbeendbare Erfahrung, zu der die minimalistischen Objekte durch ihren Entzug verführen, als genuin ästhetische erläutern. Dass und wie die minimalistischen Objekte und in deren Gefolge heute die installativen Werke auf den Betrachter bezogen sind, erfolgt mithin nicht aus kunstfremden Motiven heraus, sondern im Gegenteil im vollen Anspruch auf deren Ästhetizität. Es ist deshalb kein Wunder, dass die zeitgenössische Kunst immer wieder auch auf die historische Minimal Art zurückgeht und deren Funktionsweise erneut einsetzt. In diesem Zusammenhang ist auch Liam Gillicks *Applied Resignation Platform* zu sehen, eine 1999 für den Frankfurter Kunstverein entstandene Arbeit, für die er in einem der oberen Räume die opak weißen Glasscheiben der Oberlichtkonstruktion durch farbiges Plexiglas ersetzt hat. Die unter anderem auf die Oberflächen von Donald Judd anspielende Installation ist als Dauerleihgabe im Kunstverein geblieben; deren Ausstellung, Abbau oder Transformation liegt seitdem im Ermessen der nachfolgend gezeigten KünstlerInnen. Es entspricht der Logik von Cerith Wyn Evans´ respektvoller Arbeit mit historischen und in diesem Fall auch: zeitgenössischen Vorgängern, dass er diesen Ball aufgenommen und Gillicks bunte Plexiglasscheiben durch transparentes Glas ersetzt hat.

Das Ergebnis integriert sich stimmig in die Ausstellung. Nicht nur erinnern die nun hinter dem Glas sichtbaren Neonröhren wie auch die Deckenkonstruktion aus Beton an die einen Stock tiefer gezeigten Neonarbeiten (*Moebius Strip* und *Slow fade to black (reversed)*); auch

---

05 VGL. MICHAEL FRIED: „KUNST UND OBJEKTHAFTIGKEIT", A.A.O. DAZU: JULIANE REBENTISCH: *ÄSTHETIK DER INSTALLATION*, FRANKFURT AM MAIN 2003, BES. S. 40-81.

wirft diese Arbeit buchstäblich neues Licht auf die im selben Raum sowie an anderen Stellen des Hauses in vorderhand traditioneller Weise präsentierten Fotografien von Wyn Evans´ Vater Sulwyn. Sie erscheinen nicht mehr als in sich geschlossene Werke, sondern öffnen sich auf das installative Arrangement, in das sie eingelassen sind; sie werden Teil jenes großen, seine einzelnen Elemente vielfach untereinander vernetzenden Werkes, als das sich die Frankfurter Ausstellung insgesamt fügt. Der Titel etwa, den Evans den physiognomischen Holzstudien seines Vaters gegeben hat, *Anthropomorphic Portraits*, setzt diese mit dem eigentümlichen Anthropomorphismus der nebenan installierten Kronleuchter in Verbindung. Wie bei jenen bleibt dieser hier nämlich ebenfalls in der Latenz: ob das Holz sich mit anthropomorphen Eigenschaften maskiert, die es nicht wirklich hat oder umgekehrt einen anthropomorphen Kern unter seinen dinghaften Holzoberflächen verbirgt, ist nicht entscheidbar; unsere Erfahrung oszilliert auch hier zwischen einer immer schon mit Bedeutung durchsetzten Buchstäblichkeit und einer sich stets wieder ins Buchstäbliche zurücknehmenden Bedeutung. In dieser Weise kommunizieren die in der Ausstellung gezeigten Fotografien des biologischen Vaters auch mit den Werken der in der Ausstellung verschiedentlich zitierten intellektuellen Vaterfiguren. Wie diese lassen sie sich überdies aber auch als Hinweis auf die persona des Künstlers lesen. In einem der Fotos taucht er denn auch explizit auf: als Kind. Natürlich lässt sich aber diese Geste biografischer Selbstinszenierung nicht einfach zu den Akten einer das Werk erklärenden Künstlerlegende legen. So werden die väterlichen Fotos in der Ausstellung mit einem Wandtext konterkariert, der Zweifel an der dokumentarischen Beweiskraft früher Fotografien weckt. Was in der frühen Astrofotografie als Sonnensystem oder Galaxie identifiziert wurde, so lernen wir da, sei in Wahrheit häufig nichts anderes gewesen als die Spur von Staubpartikeln oder Schuppen, die sich in die Entwicklerflüssigkeit gemischt hatten. Freilich liegt das Spiel von Schein und Sein, das Wyn Evans in seinen Arbeiten durch Anspielungen auf seine private und professionelle Biografie in Gang setzt, nicht auf dieser medientechnischen Ebene. Dennoch vermag sich auch hier, trotz indexikalisch klarer Verhältnisse und historisch deutlicher Bezüge, keine endgültige Evidenz herzustellen, wird der Schein der Inszenierung nie auf das Sein der Person hin durchsichtig. Als Emblem einer künstlerischen Selbstinszenierung, die sich nicht von einer Tiefenhermeneutik der Künstlerintention dienstbar machen lässt, mag man auch *Future Anterior* verstehen, eine angeblich mit einer phosphorhaltigen Flüssigkeit bewässerte Orchidee, klischeehaftes Inbild des Dandykünstlers, in dessen leerer Tiefe jedoch nichts als die Projektionen des Betrachters im Kommen bleiben.

Die im Look der überaus eleganten Ausstellung auch sonst spürbare Sensibilität des Dandys – „Masque ou décor, salut! J´adore ta beauté", sagt Baudelaire[06] – provoziert jedoch nicht ein Lob der als solche zu genießenden Oberfläche, sondern eine Erfahrung, die den Betrachter wieder und wieder reflexiv auf sich und seine projektiven Kräfte zurückwirft. In und durch die Erfahrung der Werke wird der Betrachter nicht zuletzt mit sich selbst konfrontiert; denn seine eigene Bedeutungsproduktion ist es, die ihm an den Werken im verfremdenden Modus des ästhetischen Scheins entgegentritt. *Inverse Reverse Perverse* lautet Wyn Evans´ Titel für ein großes, konkaves Spiegelobjekt, dessen Schliff sich an der Krümmung der menschlichen Linse orientiert und dessen Radius den zuletzt von Le Corbusier standardisierten Maßen eines durchschnittlichen Menschen entspricht. Dieses Objekt reflektiert den sich im Raum bewegenden Betrachter, und zwar in einer rechts und links und oben und unten verkehrenden, sowie, umso deutlicher je näher man dem Objekt kommt, auch leicht verzerrenden Weise. Es reiht sich damit in die Reihe jener installativen Arbeiten ein, die seit den mittleren sechziger Jahren im Medium der Kunst explizit auf die konstitutive Rolle reflektieren, die der Betrachter für den ästhetischen Status der Werke selbst einnimmt. Die ästhetische Verflechtung

---

[06] CHARLES BAUDELAIRE, „TABLEAUX PARISIENS", IN : DERS.: *LES FLEURS DU MAL/DIE BLUMEN DES BÖSEN*, STUTTGART 1980. S. 206.

mit dem Werk aber bedeutet für den Betrachter selbst, auch dies wird an *Inverse Reverse Perverse* thematisch, ebenfalls theatralisiert zu werden. In den Prozess der ästhetischen Erfahrung einzutreten heißt, von der Bühnenpräsenz der Werke – ihrer unentscheidbaren Doppelpräsenz als Ding und als Zeichen – umgriffen, angesteckt, selbst auf die Bühne geschickt: zum Schauspieler zu werden, der deren gespanntes Verhältnis performativ austrägt. Gerade weil das Verhältnis zum Werk wesentlich unbestimmt ist, weder in einer symbolischen Bedeutung noch in der Positivität der Form sicheren Halt findet, wird der Betrachter auf seinen Part, seine Rolle in diesem Verhältnis reflektieren, auf das, was er, er allein, in dieser Situation tut. Die ästhetische Erfahrung realisiert sich mithin in einer reflexiven Unterbrechung unseres gewöhnlichen Zugangs zu den Dingen, in einer die Selbstevidenz unserer kulturellen und sozialen Hintergrundannahmen, wenn man so will, *pervertierenden* Distanznahme von der Normalität unserer alltäglichen Welthabe. Eben in dieser reflexiven, jeden unmittelbar verstehenden ebenso wie jeden bloß kulinarisch-konsumistischen Zugang verwehrenden Distanz, in der wir zu den ästhetisch erfahrenen Objekten gehalten werden, liegt, so meine ich, auch ein Moment des Widerstands der Kunst gegen die Ware, des Bilds gegen das Visuelle, des Theaters gegen das Spektakel.

Wie um mit diesem Potenzial des Ästhetischen dem Projekt der Spektakel- und Kulturindustriekritiker Debord und Adorno die Treue zu halten, sind sie es, die im Zentrum jener Arbeiten stehen, welche die Ausstellung im Foyer des Kunstvereins eröffnen und beschließen. Am Treppenaufgang hat Evans einen kreisförmig geschlossenen roten Neonschriftzug aufgehängt, der das lateinische Palindrom zitiert, das Guy Debord als Titel für einen seiner letzten Filme gewählt hat: *In Girum Imus Nocte Et Consumimur Igni* – Wir irren des Nachts im Kreis umher und werden vom Feuer verzehrt. An der Seite morst eine schlichte moderne Lampe Adornos Flaschenpost.

MANFRED HERMES
THIS DOUBLE GROUND OF SPACE: TEXT, TRANSLATION, AND BREATHING – INTERVIEW WITH CERITH WYN EVANS

THERE IS A BASIC TENSION IN MANY OF YOUR WORKS THAT I WOULD LIKE TO DESCRIBE WITH THE FOLLOWING ADJECTIVES: ISOLATED AND REFERENTIAL, REDUCTIONISTIC AND LAYERED, FACTUAL AND METAPHORIC, COLD AND DENSE.

This "tension" is sought after on one level, to establish, or rather occasion, in the viewer a familiar doubt. The relational is everything here. William Burroughs talks of "ports of entry" – a figure of multiple approaches. I am conscious of the extent I can influence and manipulate the context in which a work is placed. Often very small or seemingly insignificant shifts in the temporal, textual or spatial scheme have a profound bearing on what is understood as perceived, and how that perception is revealed. The perception of space is over-determined by the perception of time, image *through* text, and vice versa. This may be perceived by some as unnecessarily complex and perverse but that's what forms the proportions of the work. Wrong footing is part of the operating mode.

YOU WORK WITH A VAST SCOPE OF REFERENCES THAT CAN LEAVE A VIEWER WITH THE AMBIGUOUS FEELING OF BEING SLIGHTLY DISADVANTAGED.

No one is singular in this respect and I am hardly the "master" of the references myself. I never know if the references I allude to or produce have any equivalence. Their values change constantly; some become more important than others, some just fade away. Things take a value in relation to each other like floating signifiers; it's a permissiveness that comes from being a fan. I am not highly responsible. I am a magpie, a pillager of different things. I run in and steal and run away again into the arms of something else and I am never quite sure where that's going to lead me. This notion of permissiveness, of picking this or that, will probably define me as something tantamount to a historical flaneur or dilettante. Yet I am somehow bound up in this idea of selection, of sensibility, of the things that I feel "speak" to me.

THERE IS A NOTION OF APPROPRIATION IN YOUR WORK, BUT THE ISOLATED AND RECONTEXTUALIZED OBJECT OR IMAGE SEEMS TO BE OVER DETERMINED BY AN ATMOSPHERIC APPROACH.

I suppose it's a kind of an inverse notion of what has been developed since early modernism, since the idea of collage in Cubism, since this notion of taking things which are widely available from popular culture and making them part of new material. I would negotiate what is allowed within that. For me, it is more "natural" to engage with a dialogue that is already mediated. The notion of the "always already" is very present for me.

In the work that I make, I am often confronted by notions of propriety in terms of the ethics of citation. Possibly it is perceived that I don't respect the proper nouns of the author – that there is a certain laissez-faire approach to just plucking them out of the air and bringing them into an equation and trying to do something with that. It strikes me as a little bit odd when people feel that what I am trying to do is to create some dissonance or noise in terms of categories and references, further complicated by the fact that what is at stake is the right to quote someone.

IS THERE A DESIRE FOR A COMMUNAL RELATION OR A FORMATION OF SOME KIND OF IMAGINARY BAND THAT SPREADS ACROSS TIME?

If we put together all the people I touch upon (or invoke) in a lot of works they wouldn't, or couldn't, want to be part of the same band, but that doesn't prevent (in fact it may encourage) the fantasy of some imagined correspondence. Very few of us are the kind of initiates willing to go together, like Acéphale, to that special place and act out a fantasy life which is quite highly developed in terms of its symbolic codes and its notions of freedom and intimacy, the romantic notion of abandon, the summoning of "liquid" hierarchies.

OFTEN YOU REFER TO ELITIST GROUPS OR POSITIONS, THE SITUATIONISTS, BRION GYSIN OR THE ONE BEING DESCRIBED IN *LE BAPHOMET*. EARLY ACCOUNTS OF SITUATIONISM SPEAK OF "TRACES" AND "PHANTOMS". GREIL MARCUS DREW A LINE BETWEEN HISTORICAL MOMENTS OF INTENSITY SPREAD

ACROSS TIME FROM DADA TO PUNK. IS THIS NOTION OF SECRECY, OF A HIDDEN PATH, SOMETHING YOU ARE INTERESTED IN?

Not really. I'm holding up a mirror to these things because I think that the reflection evoked is captivating and worthwhile to interrogate at this point.

IS THERE A SOCIAL IDEA YOU ARE PROJECTING? ARE YOU INVOLVED IN NOTIONS OF THE SACRAL, AN ATHEOLOGICAL RELIGIOSITY IN ANY WAY?

The society of Acéphale was tiny, just a few friends, a strange experiment to push the boundaries of Surrealism as Bataille and the others had been excised by Breton at that time. The notion of Acéphale, a headless Vitruvian figure, symbolizes absolute relentless desire. The figure that is holding a dagger and a flaming heart, with death's head in place of genitals, represents a notion of pure pleasure, of absolute abandon and desire. I came to recall the Acéphale figure as a result of witnessing the horrors of the bombing of the World Trade Center. It was a response to this shock, paranoia, this absolutely terrible event – and a fantastic libidinal expenditure at the same time. Acéphale, the headless agency of pure pleasure and terror, pain and excess, was made into this cold blue, obscene neon figure and put in a gallery combined it with the Warhol silver pillows (which we were kindly given permission to quote by the Warhol Foundation) floating from the ceiling, reflecting the neon sculpture. It's all encrypted in that process somehow.[01] Encryption is an important issue here; the notion of a cipher communicating is very present. I'm often involved in discussions about how the work should be labelled, what kind of hermeneutics we can place into the discussions so that people don't feel

---

[01] THE ACÉPHALE GROUP ALSO PUBLISHED A MAGAZINE OF THE SAME TITLE. FOUR EDITIONS OF WHAT WAS BASICALLY A NIETZSCHE FANZINE APPEARED BETWEEN 1936 AND 1939. AS WELL AS GEORGES BATAILLE, PIERRE KLOSSOWSKI, MICHEL LEIRIS, ROGER CALLOIS CONTRIBUTED TO IT. MOST OF THE MAGAZINES ILLUSTRATIONS WERE DONE BY ANDRÉ MASSON, AMONGST THEM THE DRAWING OF THE HEADLESS FIGURE THAT EVANS' SCULPTURE REFERS TO.

confused or alienated, or think that there is some "in" joke happening for the very few people that can understand what's going on. I consider what is at stake in making these decisions that "frame" the work and its reception.

YOU REFUSE GIVING GENRE TO, OR BRANDING YOUR WORK BY CALLING IT INSTALLATION, FOR INSTANCE?

Yes, in part because that is something I feel is not necessary. I value the freedom I have to cite, to "channel" voices under the rubric of my practice, to somehow play with the legitimacy of my name. It is worth remembering that the title of the exhibition at the Kunstverein, which is ironic, is my name in inverted commas – "Cerith Wyn Evans" is the title of the show, which hopefully does not seem like a complete arsehole thing to do. I hope people can see that there is a certain lightness and humour to it.

NOT WANTING TO DECIDE FOR A SHOW TITLE HAD A REASON?

I had to come up with a "title", and I thought: "Oh, God. Where do you begin?" The set of references becomes like an endless chain. In this very Klossowskian way there is this notion of the dematerialisation of the proper noun.
In his novel *Le Baphomet*, characters assume the physical presence of breaths so this notion of breathing, of something far less tangible comes into play. Coming up with a title for this show – which is a survey of some works produced over the last ten years, or so seemed to imply, is too much to sum up the space of a few words.
In other words, no title "came to me" at this time.

YOUR SHOW IS A MELANCHOLIC TOUR THROUGH A HISTORY OF YOUR FASCINATIONS, INTERESTS AND INVOLVEMENTS.

I feel unable or unwilling to speak for my own singular subjective position under my own name, under the rubric that is my own identity. This idea of citation is very attractive, of calling upon others to speak on my behalf through collage and editing, because I'm somehow very narcissistically invested in that process and I feel as if I am allowed to do that as an artist. Klossowski is a good model because of his double life as writer, esoteric pornographer, and translator. I am interested in an imaginary séance of intertexts, of conjuring up in a way that Klossowski does so eloquently in *The Baphomet*; he brings in Nietzsche or Bernini and they somehow sit at the same table and have a conversation. My work is about the notion of invocation – staged – a *mise en scène* for the possibility of bringing in third voices, or other presences that appeal to me.

ONE OF THE FIRST PIECES YOU PRODUCED FOR AN ART SPACE WAS A HUGE CONCAVE MIRROR.
It was the first piece I showed at White Cube gallery[02]. It was a self-conscious thing. What could in fact be more self-conscious than fabricating a mirror? I felt that this was somehow an appropriate statement. It ended up being this idea to do with the text from which White Cube ironically takes its title: Brian O'Doherty's *Inside the White Cube*. So the idea of playing around with that was a little bit like "okay, we are trying to do something here which inverts literally, optically, perceptually the room." The viewer is on the ceiling, upside down, the perception of the self in the room is inverted. In this small gallery, the volume of the space in Duke Street St. James' in London was literally a cube. Being in Mayfair, in one of the most exclusive, highly gentrified areas where most artefacts on display in the local shops and galleries appear to conform to the status of objects in their "proper" place, it seemed okay to just play with this idea a little bit and it was – to my mind – successful from that point of view.

WHY DID YOU CHOOSE "INVERSE, REVERSE, PERVERSE" FOR A TITLE?
Not only did it describe the workings of the mirror, but it is a line from a Velvet Underground song called *The Gift*. The lyrics were

02 INVERSE REVERSE PERVERSE, WHITE CUBE / JAY JOPLING, LONDON 1996

written by John Cale, who grew up in the same village as my paternal grandparents in Garnant, South Wales. I can go on with these kinds of trails that lead to different places. This song is dedicated to notions of perversion related to Sacher-Masoch, so there is a universe whereby my grandparents in a small Welsh village, which also produced John Cale, were somehow implicated in the world of contracts between Sacher-Masoch and his mistress Wanda. It becomes this maze of references, of spiralling on and on.

YOU ARE VERY INVENTIVE IN INTRODUCING UNUSUAL MEDIA LIKE FIREWORKS, DIFFERENT LIGHT EMITTERS, PLANTS ETC.
This happens as a consequence of stumbling onto an idea and just thinking "how could a text be carried now?". Quite often the work that I make is actually just the Yellow Pages, a repository for production. I also rely on a whole community of different people. Every show I do I take it a little step further. I have a notebook, which is a very slim volume of things that I have never done before. I've never done wallpaper. Wallpaper would be something I'd like to do. I had never done a slide projection until my last show[03] – a notion of dissolving and breathing in and out, the complexity and density of what an image and the materiality of the image are, of what symbolic identification the pictures might bear and bring into a room.

DID IT FEEL LIKE A BREAK FROM THE FILM AND VIDEO WORK TO PRODUCE WORK FOR AN ART SPACE?
No, it didn't. I studied sculpture at art school, which really seemed like an expanded field. Then I studied film at the Royal College of Art, but considered those distinctions always as quite limiting. I was constantly in trouble because I was in someone else's class trying to shift across the boundaries a little bit. But what was probably more important was my teaching. I've done a lot of teaching over the years, and that really informed the way in which I approach making work. I taught for six

[03] THE SKY IS AS THIN AS PAPER HERE, GALERIE BUCHHOLZ, COLOGNE 2004

years at the Architectural Association in London, which I never had a real place to be at because I never qualified as an architect in any sense. But fortunately because it was student-led, there were enough people kind enough to support me in their curiosity. So I'd run a film programme or get someone in to talk about how tailoring was made, or how to cut a jacket, things I felt were important to influence the concept of architecture, things I felt were interesting from the margins of what architecture or graphic design could be. A whole class did choreography with Michael Clarke for a term; students attended ballet classes every day. It was hugely important and rewarding for me that people took my approach seriously.

SO YOU DO RELY ON A VERY OPEN, INTERDISCIPLINARY TYPE OF CREATIVITY.

I really do. I don't know whether this would come across as "unprofessional." My work ethic is highly critical of an "anything goes" liberalism. John Cage is a great example here: absolutely *not* anything goes. Anything *but* anything goes, actually.

THERE IS VERY MUCH AN "ANYTHING GOES" SITUATION RIGHT NOW WHEN SIXTY PER CENT OF A SHOW CAN CONSIST OF VIDEO INSTALLATIONS. VIDEO TRANSCENDS A GIVEN SPACE INTO SOME TV-TYPE EXPERIENCE TAKING YOU SOMEWHERE ELSE. ONE CAN RELATE THAT NEGATIVELY TO WHAT YOU DO, HAVING WORKED WITH MOVING IMAGES AND GOING ON TO PRODUCE A DIFFERENT RANGE OF WORK - AND PROJECT *THAT* INTO EXISTING SPACES.

There is this assumption that the image is what happens within the screen. People think that emotional and symbolic or representational content is something that only happens within a picture. I was always more interested in the structural, material aspects – what the notion of projection means. I want to knock on the walls or look at the materiality of how this is translated into pixels or the grain of emulsion, how the image is even possible. That's not really the opposite, but it is like Julia Kristeva put it: "Enough of the signifier, give me the signified." So there is a reversal: show me were the meaning is, the drives; show me where the doubt is, show me where they are and how they are made articulate in a constellation of projection and introjection.

A LOT OF YOUR WORK CAN STILL BE RELATED TO A NOTION OF THE CINEMATIC, THOUGH.

The succession of images and the production of a succession of images are something captivating to me, and there is nothing in the exhibition which isn't that in a funny way. Even though it might appear just like objects placed in a room, the exhibition is a film. I'm interested in the notion of *mise en scène*. I am acutely aware of how much time it takes to walk up the staircase and what you see first and what the sightlines are into another room. I think of this as a temporal extension of what the choices are to turn left or right and what develops out of that. I very consciously thought of it as a ... narrative wouldn't be an accurate way of describing how I think about it, but there is a progression of images, of spatial affinities. There is a beginning, a middle and an end, which in this case you have to reverse again in order to leave from the beginning – so, a loop of sorts.

HOW DO YOU START CONCEIVING YOUR SPACES OR AMBIENCES? DOES THE INVOLVEMENT START WITH A COMMISSION, AND THEN DEVELOP ALONG THE LINES OF WHAT YOU THINK COULD BE FITTING IN A GIVEN SITUATION?

Quite often it is about this idea of taking a sentence in a book or a line of poetry or a picture in a magazine into time and space to producing something that finally comes under the auspice of my name and becomes something differently configured in the world.

IN THE CASE OF THIS SHOW, THE GIVENS ARE THE FRANKFURTER KUNSTVEREIN. BUT IT'S NOT ONLY THIS PARTICULAR SITE, AS YOUR SHOW IS BASICALLY A RETROSPECTIVE.

That's a bit strange for me because I am more familiar and accustomed with moving from place to place and making something accurate to that moment and place in time. Actively, like a musician making a performance I appreciate that it happens within a given time. So when the cupboards are open and you go into the old stuff and bring that into a space with more recent things it's also nerve-racking.

The question was how to adapt things which have existed in many different situations to this place; it's like having two givens that multiply, like seeing if those two givens most sympathetically can respond to each other.

THERE ARE TENDENCIES TO INDULGE IN ROMANTIC IMAGERY, IN NOCTURNAL AND UNIVERSALIST MOTIFS.

In my last show I wanted to bring into the space through images a certain very coded, or pointed, notion of the exotic other – Japanese naked boys and, from an equally reduced book from the 1960s, astronomical photographs. So simply by choosing these two books and blending the images of the "naked festivals" in Japan, this great bacchanalia, with images of the universe, there is this impossibility of imagining where and how that could be and the incapacity that technology has for being able to realize the real. Blending these two things together was, in a way, a romantic gesture.

THE UNIVERSE TURNED OUT TO BE "AS THIN AS PAPER" THERE.

It is about moving through paper into some other puncture. "The sky is thin as paper here" is actually a quote from William Burroughs, where he talks about a band of cowboys who accidentally fire off a gun in a cemetery in Boulder, Colorado in Eighteen-thirty something. They shoot a hole through the sky whereupon they realize that their reality is in fact a fabrication; that they are actually on stage.

YOU PRODUCE AMBIENCES THAT WORK IN A DECIDEDLY SCARCE MANNER, OFTEN RESULTING IN A SOMEWHAT GLASSY, KUBRICK-LIKE ELEGANCE.

When you actually place the works in a space they perform and become highly charged, but for me it is never a straightforward thing. It's this closure of something I resist.

BUT YOUR WORK TAKES THIS PARTICULAR PHYSICAL FORM AND IT MIGHT NOT ALWAYS BE EASY TO GET BEYOND INITIAL MISPERCEPTIONS. THEN YOU GET MORE INVOLVED IN THOSE RESONATING,

RICHLY LAYERED STRUCTURES, BUT THAT IT DOESN'T MEAN THAT IT WILL HAVE AN EFFECT IN AN INTERVIEW-TYPE SITUATION.

Effect is a good word. Maurice Merleau-Ponty uses the word "occasion". I find it very moving when he says: It occasions in someone. I think this is an elegant and an extraordinary notion that something can be occasioned in another person. It's a projection into another person's reality that's there. Merleau-Ponty speaks so well about this double ground of space in *The Visible and the Invisible*. He says: "How are we to name, to describe, such as I see it from my place, that *lived by another* which yet for me is not nothing, since I believe in the other – and that which furthermore concerns me myself, since it is there as another's view upon me? Here is this well-known countenance, this smile, these modulations of voice, whose style is as familiar to me as myself. Perhaps in many moments of my life the other is for me reduced to this spectacle, which can be a charm. But should the voice alter, should unwonted appear in the score of the dialogue, or, on the contrary, should a response respond too well to what I thought without having really said it – and suddenly there breaks forth the evidence that yonder also, minute by minute, life is being lived: somewhere behind those eyes, behind those gestures, or rather before them, or again about them, coming from I know not what double ground of space, another private world shows through, through the fabric of my own, and for a moment I live in it; I am no more than the respondent for the interpellation that is made to me. To be sure, the least recovery of attention persuades me that this other who invades me is made only of my own substance; how could I conceive, precisely as *his*, *his* colours, *his* pain, *his* world, except as in accordance with the colours I see, the pains I have had, the world wherein I live? But at least my private world has ceased to be mine only; it is now the instrument which another plays, the dimension of a generalised life which is grafted onto my own."[04]

That's an amazing passage in the last, unfinished book he wrote that almost vanishes into nothing – the text "literally" dematerialises.

He talks about a transitivity between bodies of the same type which somehow negotiates the space not only between the particular and the general, but also between the particular and the particular and the general and the general. Merleau-Ponty takes it from a phenomenological real of a body in space into a conjecture which could actually make a community possible, could actually make a correspondence possible and real on a different level. Later on we find:
"There is a circle of the touched and the touching, the touched takes hold of the touching; there is a circle of the visible and the seeing, the seeing is not without visible existence; there is even an inscription of the touching in the visible, of the seeing in the tangible – and the converse; there is finally a propagation of these exchanges to all the bodies of the same type and of the same style which I see and touch – and this by virtue of the fundamental fission or segregation of the sentient and the sensible which, laterally, makes the organs of my body communicate and founds transitivity from one body to another."[05] That there is this transitivity between bodies, races, styles, and fundamental concepts of "otherness" melts down in this idea. I think that there is a highly sophisticated, highly optimistic, almost utopian form of correspondence.

---

04 MAURICE MERLEAU-PONTY: *THE VISIBLE AND THE INVISIBLE*, ED. BY CLAUDE LEFORT, TRANS. ALPHONSO LINGIS (NORTHWESTERN UNIVERSITY PRESS, EVANSTON, 1968), 11F

05 IBID, 143.

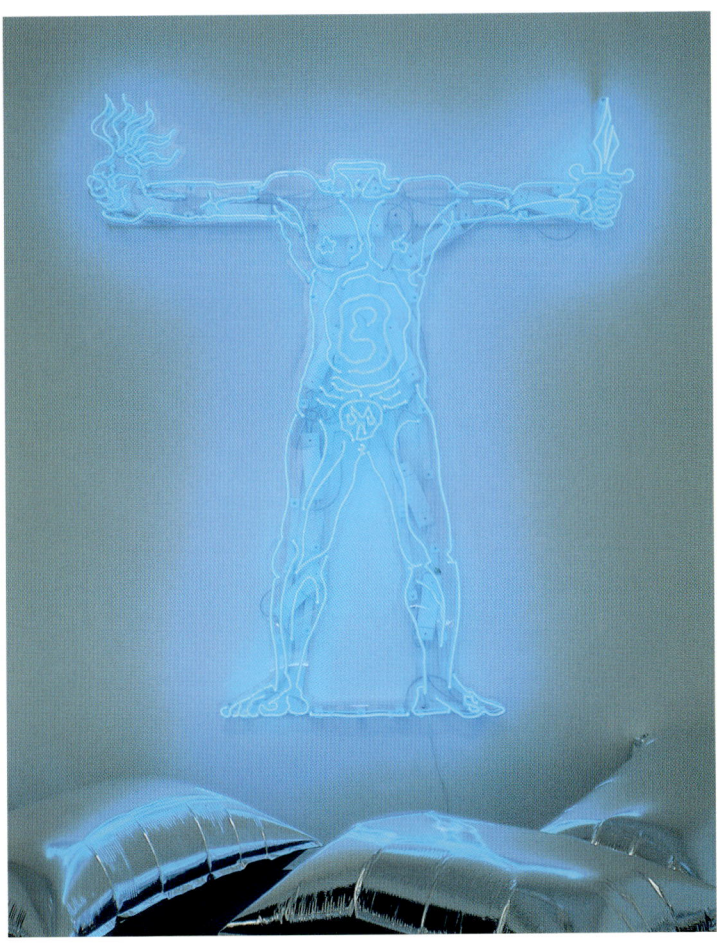

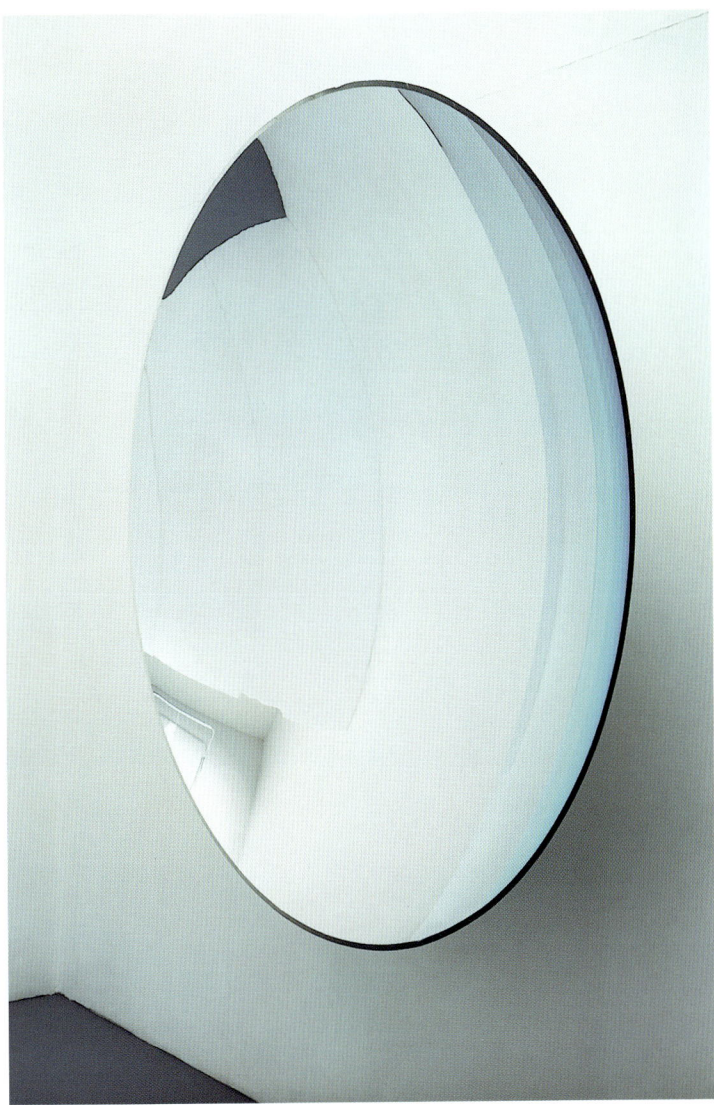

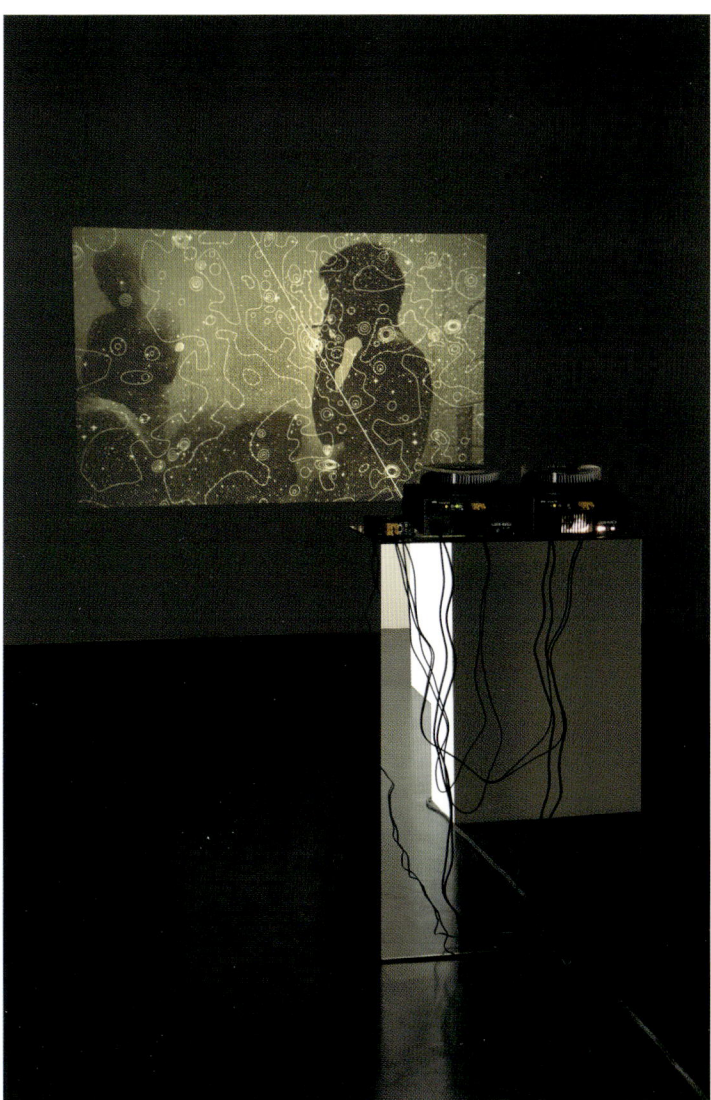

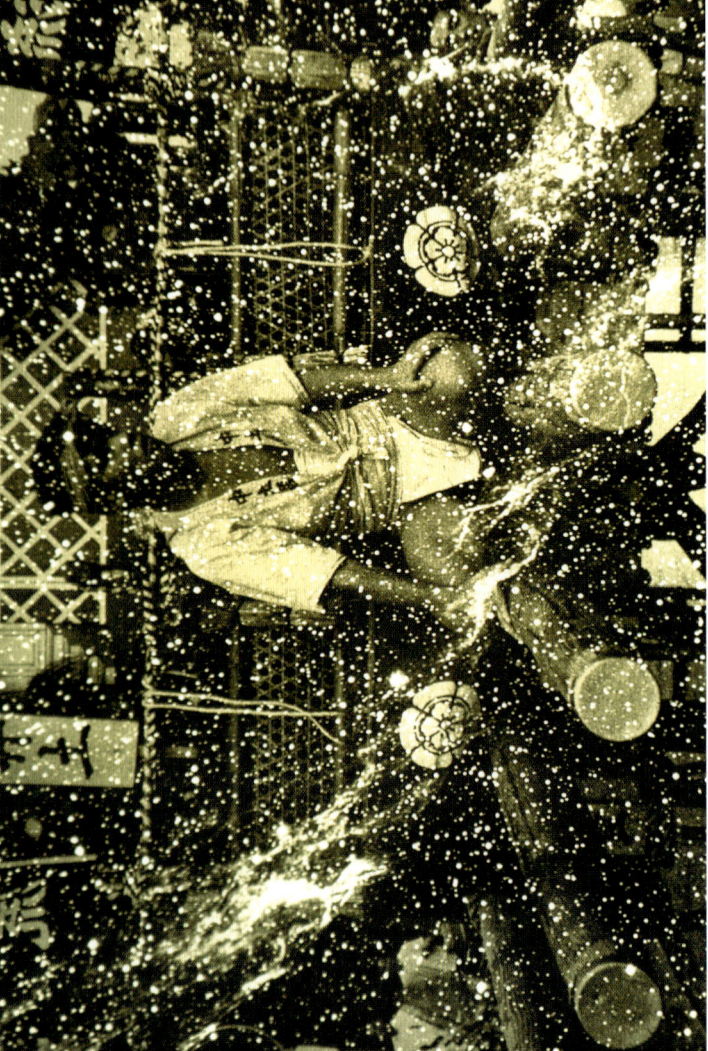

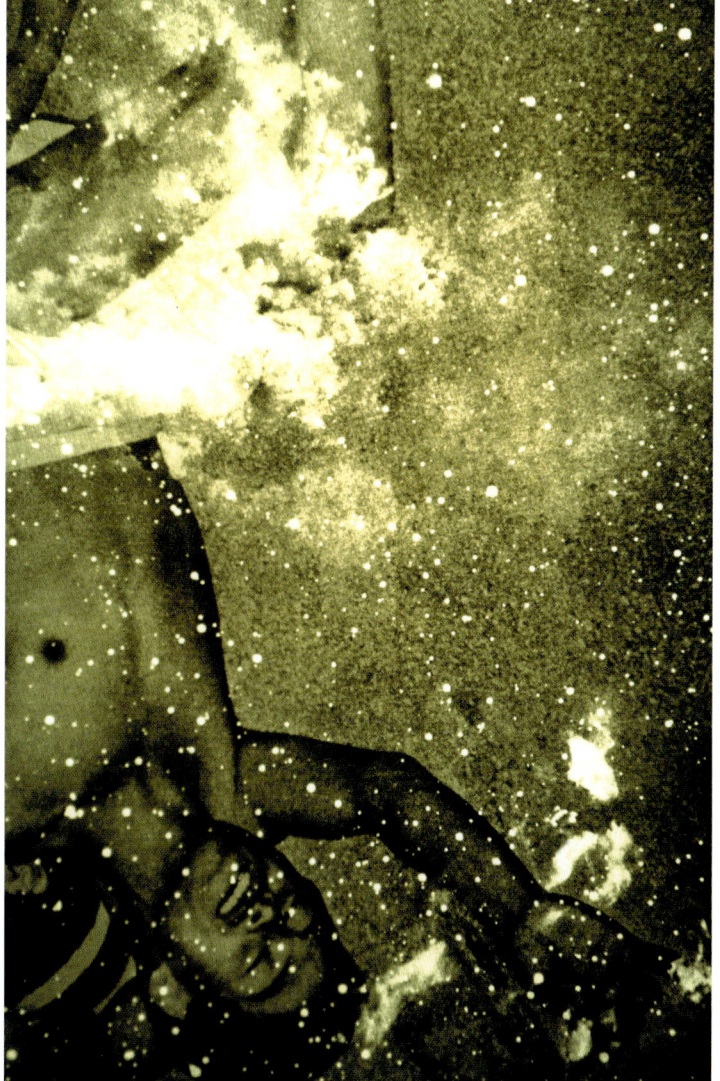

Acephale, 2001
Neon, electronic construction, 180 x 150 cm
Collection DekaBank, Frankfurt am Main

Inverse Reverse Perverse, 1996
Surface mirrored acrylic, 173 cm diameter
Installation view White Cube / Jay Jopling

The sky is thin as paper here... (Slide projection), 2004
2 Slide projectors (1. projector: 28 slides, 2. projector: 32 slides), dissolver, mirror mounted pedestal
Installation view Galerie Daniel Buchholz, Cologne

The sky is thin as paper here... (Slide projection), 2004 (detail)

The sky is thin as paper here... (Slide projection), 2004 (detail)

The sky is thin as paper here.... (neon), 2004
Neon text, perspex, ca. 18 x 200 cm
Installation view Galerie Daniel Buchholz, Cologne

MANFRED HERMES
DIESE DOPPELBÖDIGKEIT DES RAUMS: TEXT, ÜBERSETZUNG, ATMEN – INTERVIEW MIT CERITH WYN EVANS

ES GIBT IN DEINEN ARBEITEN EINE SPANNUNG, DIE ICH MIT DEN FOLGENDEN ADJEKTIVEN BESCHREIBEN MÖCHTE: ISOLIERT UND REFERENZIELL, REDUKTIONISTISCH UND GESCHICHTET, FAKTISCH UND METAPHORISCH, KÜHL UND DICHT.

Diese „Spannung" wird auf einer bestimmten Ebene sicherlich gesucht. Im Betrachter soll ein Zweifel des vertraut Ungewissen ausgelöst oder geradezu geschürt werden. Beziehungen sind hier alles. William Burroughs spricht von „Eintrittspforten", was eine Vielzahl von Zugängen impliziert. Ich bin mir durchaus über den Radius im Klaren, auf den ich zugreifen und innerhalb dessen ich Zusammenhänge beeinflussen kann. Dabei können unscheinbare Umschichtungen im zeitlichen, textlichen oder räumlichen Gefüge die weitreichendsten Folgen haben sowohl für das Verständnis des Wahrgenommenen als auch seine Hervorbringung. Es gibt eine Überdeterminierung der Raum- durch die Zeitwahrnehmung, des Bildes *durch* den Text und umgekehrt. Das mag einigen unnötig komplex und pervers erscheinen, bestimmt aber die Verhältnisse der Produktion. Jemanden auf dem falschen Fuß zu erwischen ist ein Teil meiner Arbeitsweise.

DU DECKST EINE UNGLAUBLICHE BREITE AN REFERENZEN AB. DAS KANN IM BETRACHTER DAS GEFÜHL LEICHTER BENACHTEILIGUNG BEWIRKEN.

In dieser Hinsicht gibt es keine Einzigartigkeit und ich selbst bin keineswegs der „Meister der Referenzen". Ich weiß selbst nie, ob die Bezüge, auf die ich anspiele oder die ich herstelle, irgendeine wirkliche Entsprechung haben. Ihre Wertigkeit ändert sich ständig: Einiges wird wichtiger, anderes verblasst ganz einfach. Dinge bekommen einen Wert durch die Beziehung, in der sie zueinander stehen. Meine Nachgiebigkeit hat immer auch mit Fan-Sein zu tun. Ich bin nicht besonders verantwortungsbewusst. Ich bin eine Elster, ein Plünderer verschiedenster Dinge. Ich stürme rein, klaue etwas und laufe davon, in die Arme von etwas anderem, und ich bin selbst nie ganz sicher, wohin mich das führt. Diese Freiheit, hier und da herumzupicken, könnte mir natürlich den Vorwurf des historischen Flaneurs oder Dilettanten

einbringen. Aber dazu glaube ich dann doch zu sehr an diese Idee der
Auswahl, der Sensibilität, daran, dass es Dinge gibt, von denen ich
fühle, dass sie zu mir „sprechen".

DEINE ARBEIT BERUHT AUF DEM PRINZIP VON ANEIGNUNG, ABER DIE ISOLIERTEN UND VERSTELLTEN OBJEKTE UND BILDER FINDEN SICH IN EINER DICHTEN ATMOSPHÄRIK WIEDER.

Vermutlich geht es hier um die Umkehrung einer Auffassung, die in
der Frühzeit der Moderne entwickelt wurde, vor allem durch die ku-
bistische Collage: sich Dinge, die als Teil der Populärkultur weithin
verfügbar sind, anzueignen und aus ihnen etwas Neues zu machen.
Das ist der Rahmen, in dem ich die Verhandlungen über das Erlaubte
und Mögliche führe. Es kommt mir „natürlicher" vor, mich in einen
Dialog zu stellen, der bereits vermittelt ist. Das Immer-schon ist für
mich allgegenwärtig. Während meiner Arbeit stellen sich oft Fragen
nach der Angemessenheit im Sinne einer Ethik des Zitats. Möglich,
dass das als Respektlosigkeit gegenüber dem „Namen des Autors"
erscheint. Aber es geht hier auch um eine entspannte Art, Dinge einfach aus der Luft zu greifen, sie in eine Gleichung zu stellen und zu
sehen, was dann geschieht. Ich habe es immer etwas seltsam ge-
funden, dass Leute annehmen, mir ginge es nur darum, Dissonanzen
oder Geräusche zu produzieren, die sich auf bestimmte Kategorien
und Referenzen beziehen; und es wird noch komplizierter, wenn einem
das Recht zu zitieren überhaupt abgesprochen wird.

ES SCHEINT, ALS ÄUSSERTE SICH IN DEINER ARBEIT DER WUNSCH NACH EINER ART GEMEINSCHAFT, ALS GINGE ES UM DIE BILDUNG EINER IMAGINÄREN BAND QUER DURCH DIE ZEITEN.

Wenn man die Leute zusammenbringen würde, auf die ich in vielen
Arbeiten anspiele, dann würden sie weder zur gleichen Band gehören
können noch wollen. Das heißt aber nicht, dass man sich Überschnei-
dungen nicht vorstellen kann (und vielleicht werden sie gerade durch
die Imagination angestoßen). Aber es gibt nur sehr wenige Menschen,
die bereit wären, sich der Rolle des Einzuweihenden unterzuordnen,
wie das etwa von Acéphale gefordert wurde: Sich an einen speziellen

Ort zu begeben, um dort Fantasieakte auszuleben, die symbolischen Codes und höchst entwickelten Vorstellungen von Freiheit und Intimität folgen – also romantischen Vorstellungen von Hingabe und dem Aufrufen „fließender" Hierarchien.

DU BEZIEHST DICH OFT AUF ELITÄRE GRUPPEN ODER POSITIONEN, DIE SITUATIONISTEN, BRION GYSIN, „DER BAPHOMET". AUCH DIE FRÜHEN GESAMTDARSTELLUNGEN DES SITUATIONISMUS HABEN VON „SPUREN" AND „PHANTOMEN" GESPROCHEN. GREIL MARCUS ZOG LINIEN ZWISCHEN GESCHICHTLICHEN MOMENTEN GROSSER INTENSITÄT ETWA ZWISCHEN DADA UND PUNK. BIST DU ÄHNLICH VOM GEHEIMNIS, VON ÜBERWUCHERTEN WEGEN FASZINIERT?

Eigentlich nicht. Ich halte diesen Dingen eher den Spiegel vor, finde aber, dass diese Spiegelung sehr fesselnd ist und ein Verhör zu diesem Zeitpunkt im Übrigen lohnen sein kann.

PROJIZIERST DU EINE IDEE DES SOZIALEN – BIST DU AM SAKRALEN ODER EINER ART A-THEOLOGISCHER RELIGIOSITÄT INTERESSIERT?

Acéphale war nur eine winzige Gruppe, ein paar Freunde, die sich auf ein seltsames Experiment einließen, um die Grenzen des Surrealismus zu übertreten. Bataille und die anderen waren von Breton seinerzeit aus der Gruppe ausgeschlossen worden. Acéphale, diese kopflose vitruvianische Figur mit dem Dolch, dem brennenden Herzen und einem Totenkopf an Stelle des Genitals, steht für die reinste Form des Vergnügens, für absolute Hingabe und ein unerbittliches Begehren. Ich habe mich nach dem Angriff auf das World Trade Center wieder an diese Figur erinnert. Sie enthielt für mich eine Antwort auf den Schock und die Paranoia, die dieses schreckliche Ereignis ausgelöst hat, das ja gleichzeitig auch der Akt einer libidinösen Verausgabung von fantastischen Dimensionen war. Acéphale, dieser kopflose Vertreter des reinen Vergnügens und des Terrors, von Schmerz und Exzess, wurde bei mir zu einer kühlen, blauen, obszönen Neonfigur in einer Galerie.[01] Dort kam sie mit Warhols an der Decke schwebenden Silberkissen zusammen (die Rechte darauf wurden mir freundlicherweise von der Warhol Foundation überlassen), auf denen sich das Licht der Skulptur spiegelte. Irgendwie war das alles in diesem Vorgang verschlüsselt, wobei Verschlüsselung hier der springende Punkt ist. Die Vorstellung der kommunizierenden Chiffre ist da sehr präsent. Ich werde oft gefragt, wie man meine Arbeit nennen sollte, welche Hermeneutik man in die Diskussion werfen könnte, damit die Leute nicht zu sehr verwirrt werden, sich zurückgestoßen fühlen oder glauben, es würden da Insider-Witze abgespult, die nur wenige verstehen. Mir geht es aber eher um die Entscheidungen, die eine Arbeit und ihre Wahrnehmung „rahmen".

DU UMGEHST DIE GENRE-ZUORDNUNG ODER FESTLEGUNG DEINER ARBEIT AUCH DADURCH, DASS DU DIE BEZEICHNUNG INSTALLATION ABLEHNST.
Ja, weil ich das unnötig finde. Ich schätze die Freiheit, die ich mir nehmen kann, verschiedene Stimmen zu zitieren, unter dem Dach meiner künstlerischen Praxis zu „kanalisieren" und so auch mit der Berechtigung meines Namens zu spielen. Ich möchte an dieser Stelle darauf hinweisen, dass der – ironische – Titel der Ausstellung im Kunstverein mein Name in Anführungszeichen ist, also „Cerith Wyn Evans", was hoffentlich nicht völlig arschig wirkt. Aber ich hätte doch gern, dass eine Leichtigkeit und ein gewisser Humor erkennbar bleibt.

ES HATTE ALSO EINEN GRUND, SICH NICHT FÜR EINEN AUSSTELLUNGSTITEL ZU ENTSCHEIDEN.
Für irgendeinen „Titel" musste ich mich ja entscheiden. Da denkt man erstmal: „Oh, mein Gott. Wo fange ich an?" Jedes Bezugsfeld bildet wieder endlose Ketten. In einer sehr an Klossowski erinnernden Weise entsteht so die Idee der Entmaterialisierung des Eigennamens. In Klossowskis Roman *Der Baphomet* gehen die Figuren von der

---

01 DIE ACÉPHALE-GRUPPE BRACHTE IM ÜBRIGEN EINE GLEICHNAMIGE ZEITSCHRIFT HERAUS. ZWISCHEN 1936 UND 1939 ERSCHIENEN VIER AUSGABEN DES NIETZSCHE-FANZINES. AN DER ZEITSCHRIFT ARBEITETEN NEBEN GEORGES BATAILLE AUCH PIERRE KLOSSOWSKI, MICHEL LEIRIS, ROGER CALLOIS U.A. MIT. VON ANDRÉ MASSON STAMMEN DIE MEISTEN DER ILLUSTRATIONEN, DARUNTER AUCH DIE ZEICHNUNG DER KOPFLOSEN FIGUR, DIE VON EVANS SKULPTUR ZITIERT WIRD.

physischen Präsenz des Atems aus, so dass mit der Vorstellung des Atmens etwas viel weniger Fassbares ins Spiel kommt. Jeder andere Titel für diese Ausstellung, die immerhin einen Überblick über meine Arbeiten der letzten zehn Jahre oder so gibt, hätte die Zusammenfassung von zu viel auf zu engem Raum bedeutet. Mit anderen Worten, es kam zu jenem Zeitpunkt kein anderer Titel auf mich zu.

DEINE AUSSTELLUNG IST ALSO EINE MELANCHOLISCHE TOUR DURCH DIE JÜNGERE GESCHICHTE DEINER FASZINATIONEN, INTERESSEN UND BESCHÄFTIGUNGEN.

Ich bin völlig unfähig und eigentlich auch nicht bereit, über meine singuläre Stellung als Subjekt zu sprechen, unter meinem Namen oder der Rubrik einer Identität. Deshalb ist die Idee des Zitats für mich ja so anziehend. Auf diese Weise und durch Collage und Schnitt kann ich andere aufrufen, in meinem Namen zu sprechen. Zu einem gewissen Grad bin ich in diesen Vorgang sicher auch narzisstisch verstrickt, aber das glaube ich mir als Künstler leisten zu dürfen. Klossowski ist wegen seines Doppellebens als Schriftsteller, esoterischer Pornograf und Übersetzer auch in diesem Fall ein gutes Modell. Ich bin wie er an einer imaginären Séance von Intertexten interessiert, an der Art von Beschwörung, die er in *Der Baphomet* so beredt unternimmt, wenn er Nietzsche oder Bernini am selben Tisch zu einem Gespräch zusammenbringt. Auch in meiner Arbeit gibt es die Idee der Anrufung. Sie wird zu einer *mise en scène* dritter Stimmen und anderer Präsenzen, die mir gefallen.

EINE DEINER ERSTEN ARBEITEN FÜR DEN GALERIEBEREICH WAR EIN GROSSER KONKAVER SPIEGEL.

Das war die erste Arbeit und ich habe sie bei White Cube[02] gezeigt. Ein sehr selbstbewusstes Ding. Was könnte auch selbstbewusster als ein Spiegel sein. Ich empfand das als ein passendes Statement. Zudem spiegelte sich darin ja auch der Text, auf den sich der Name der Galerie bezieht, Brian O'Doherty's *Inside the White Cube*. Das

---

[02] INVERSE REVERSE PERVERSE, WHITE CUBE/JAY JOPLING, LONDON 1996

war natürlich ein bisschen wie „okay, jetzt versuchen wir mal, diesen Raum buchstäblich, optisch und wahrnehmungsmäßig auf den Kopf zu stellen". Der Betrachter befindet sich an der Decke, steht auf dem Kopf, die Wahrnehmung des Raumes wird verkehrt. Zudem hatte der Raum dieser kleinen Galerie in der Duke Street St. James' tatsächlich eine Würfelform. Und außerdem lag White Cube in Mayfair, einem der exklusivsten und gentrifiziertesten Stadtteile Londons, wo die meisten ausgestellten Produkte in Läden und Galerien in völliger Konformität den Status von Objekten an ihrem angemessenen Ort einnehmen. Es schien also in Ordnung, damit ein bisschen zu spielen und in dieser Hinsicht war die Ausstellung auch ein Erfolg.

KÖNNTEST DU ETWAS ÜBER DEN TITEL „INVERSE, REVERSE, PERVERSE" SAGEN?

Er beschreibt natürlich das, was der Spiegel tut, bezieht sich aber auch auf den Song „The Gift" von Velvet Underground. John Cale, der wie die Eltern meines Vaters in Garnant, South Wales, aufgewachsen ist, hat den Text geschrieben. Ich könnte mit dieser Art von Bezügen jetzt natürlich endlos weitermachen und das würde uns zu den unterschiedlichsten Orten führen. Der Song bezieht sich nicht zuletzt auf Vorstellungen von Perversion, die mit Sacher-Masoch zusammenhängen. So entsteht ein Universum, in dem meine Großeltern in einem kleinen walisischen Ort, der auch John Cale hervorgebracht hat, irgendwie in die Welt der Verträge verwickelt werden, die zwischen Sacher-Masoch und Wanda, seiner Geliebten, geschlossen wurden. Und so könnte man sich in diesem Irrgarten der Bezüge weiter und weiter drehen.

DU BIST RECHT ERFINDUNGSREICH BEI DER NUTZUNG UNGEWÖHNLICHER MATERIALIEN UND MEDIEN WIE ETWA FEUERWERK, LICHTQUELLEN, PFLANZEN.

Das passiert einfach beim Stolpern über Einfälle oder wenn ich darüber nachdenke, in welcher Form ich einen Text ausführen könnte. Dabei sind mir die Gelben Seiten sehr behilflich, sie sind meine Fundgrube für die Produktion. Ich werde natürlich auch von den unterschiedlichsten Leuten unterstützt. In jeder Ausstellung treibe ich das Spiel ein Stück weiter. Ich habe ein Notizbuch, es ist zwar sehr dünn, vermerkt aber alle Dinge, die ich noch nie gemacht habe. Ich habe noch nie Tapeten benutzt. Mit Tapeten würde ich gerne arbeiten. Ich habe nie eine Diaprojektion gemacht. Also habe ich das in meiner letzten Ausstellung versucht.[03] Ich habe das mit der Idee von Überblendung und Atmung zusammengebracht, wodurch sich in aller Komplexität und Dichte sowohl die Materialität eines Bildes zeigt wie auch die symbolische Identifikation, die Bilder tragen und in einen Raum einführen können.

WIRKTE ES EIGENTLICH WIE EIN BRUCH, VON DER FILM-/ VIDEOARBEIT ZUR KUNSTPRODUKTION ZU WECHSELN?

Nein, gar nicht. Ich habe Bildhauerei an einer Kunsthochschule studiert und das war schon ein ziemlich offenes Gebiet. Dann habe ich Film am Royal College of Art Film gemacht und da kamen mir fachliche Abgrenzungen nicht weniger einengend vor. Ich hatte allerdings ständig Ärger, weil ich mich nicht an die Regeln der Ausbildung gehalten und immer versucht habe, ein wenig die Grenzen zu verletzen. Eine viel wichtigere Rolle spielte in diesem Zusammenhang aber das Unterrichten. Ich habe ziemlich lange gelehrt und das hat meine Arbeitsweise nachhaltig geprägt. Ich war sechs Jahre an der Architectural Association in London, wo ich eigentlich nichts verloren hatte, weil ich mich nie irgendwie als Architekt hervorgetan habe. Aber glücklicherweise und weil der Unterricht von den Studenten selbst organisiert wurde, war man dort freundlich genug, mich mit einer grundsätzlichen Neugier zu unterstützen. Ich habe also Filmprogramme gemacht oder einen Schneider eingeladen, der erklärte, wie man ein Jacket zuschneidet. Also lauter Dinge, die ich für wichtig hielt, um von den Rändern her ein neues Licht auf die Möglichkeiten von Architektur oder Grafikdesign zu werfen. Eine ganze Klasse belegte für

[03] THE SKY IS THIN AS PAPER HERE..., GALERIE DANIEL BUCHHOLZ, KÖLN 2004

ein Semester Choreografie bei Michael Clark. Die Studenten kamen jeden Tag zu Ballettstunden. Es war enorm wichtig und lohnend für mich, dass mein Ansatz ernst genommen wurde.

DU BEVORZUGST ALSO DEN OFFENEN, INTERDISZIPLINÄREN KREAVITÄTSTYP?

Das tue ich wirklich. Es kann natürlich sein, dass das als „unprofessionell" gilt, andererseits steht meine Arbeitsmoral einem „alles geht"-Liberalismus durchaus kritisch gegenüber. John Cage ist hier ein großartiges Beispiel: alles andere als „alles geht". Eher schon, alles geht *außer* „alles geht".

ES GIBT AUGENBLICKLICH EINE BESONDERE ALLES-GEHT-SITUATION, WENN MAN SIEHT, WIE SECHZIG PROZENT EINER AUSSTELLUNG AUS VIDEOINSTALLATIONEN BESTEHEN KÖNNEN. VIDEO TRANSZENDIERT EINEN GEGEBENEN RAUM IN EINE TV-ARTIGE ERFAHRUNG, DIE EINEN WOANDERS HINTRÄGT. MAN KANN DAS NEGATIV AUF DEINE ARBEIT BEZIEHEN: DU HAST ZUNÄCHST MIT DEM BEWEGTEN BILD GEARBEITET UND DANN DEN SCHRITT IN EIN ANDERES ARBEITSFELD VOLLZOGEN. NUN PROJIZIERST DU DINGE *IN* EXISTIERENDE RÄUME.

Es gibt die Annahme, dass das Bild das ist, was sich innerhalb oder auf einer Leinwand ereignet. Man glaubt, dass sich emotionale, symbolische oder repräsentierende Inhalte nur innerhalb eines Bildes ereignen. Ich war aber immer eher an den strukturellen Aspekten, etwa der Projektion, interessiert. Ich möchte an die Wände klopfen, auf die Materialität eingehen und sehen, wie sich ein Bild in Pixel oder in das Korn der Emulsion übersetzt, wie das Bild überhaupt möglich wird. Das ist nicht wirklich das Gegenteil, aber es ist doch eher so, wie es Julia Kristeva gesagt hat: „Genug vom Bezeichnenden, gebt mir das Bezeichnete." Es gibt da also eine Verkehrung: Zeige mir, wo die Bedeutung ist, wo die Antriebe sind, zeige mir, wo der Zweifel sitzt und wie sich das alles in einer projektiven und introjektiven Konstellation abbilden kann.

VIELE DEINER ARBEITEN KANN MAN IMMER NOCH MIT EINER IDEE DES CINEMATISCHEN IN VERBINDUNG BRINGEN.

Bilderfolgen und ihre Herstellung fesseln mich sehr. Es gibt in dieser aktuellen Ausstellung nichts, das nicht in einer seltsamen Art auch cinematisch wäre. Wenn es auch so aussehen mag, als ginge es nur um Objekte, die in einen Raum gestellt wurden, so sind meine Ausstellungen irgendwie doch auch Filme. In die *mise en scène* bin ich sehr involviert. Mir ist völlig bewusst, wie lange man braucht, um etwa ein Treppenhaus hochzugehen, was man als erstes sieht und wie die Blickachsen und die zeitlichen Ausdehnungen verlaufen, welche Richtungswechsel möglich sind und was sich daraus wieder ergibt. Mit aller Klarheit sehe ich das als ... Erzählung wäre jetzt etwas viel gesagt, aber es entsteht eben eine Folge von Bildern und räumlichen Affinitäten. Es gibt einen Anfang, eine Mitte und ein Ende, das in diesem Fall wieder ein umgekehrtes ist, da man die Ausstellung am Ausgangspunkt verlässt – also eine Art Schleife durchläuft.

WIE BEGINNT DER AKT DER PLANUNG DIESER RÄUME? ENTWICKELT SICH DAS AUS DEM AUFTRAG, ENTLANG DER VORGABEN EINER GEGEBENEN SITUATION?

Sehr oft geht der Idee ein Satz aus einem Buch, eine Gedichtzeile oder ein Magazinfoto voraus, das dann in die Zeit und den Raum gestellt wird, um etwas zu produzieren, das schließlich unter die Schirmherrschaft meines Namens gerät und dann zu etwas anders Konfiguriertem wird.

IN DIESEM FALL GIBT ES DIE RÄUMLICHKEITEN DES FRANKFURTER KUNSTVEREINS, ANDERERSEITS IST DIESE AUSSTELLUNG VOR ALLEM EINE RETROSPEKTIVE.

Das ist für mich wirklich etwas seltsam, weil ich daran gewöhnt bin, von Ort zu Ort zu ziehen und jedes Mal für die Situation etwas genau Passendes zu produzieren. Da bin ich wie ein Musiker, der für seinen Auftritt den jeweils gegebenen Raum aktiv nutzt. Wenn also die Schränke geöffnet werden und du schaust durch dein altes Zeug und bringst das in einem Raum mit neueren Sachen zusammen, dann ist das auch nervend. Ich musste mich fragen, wie ich diese ganzen Dinge, die vorher in den verschiedensten Situationen existiert haben, aneinander anpassen werde. Ich hatte es in Frankfurt also mit zwei Gegebenheiten zu tun, die sich vervielfachen, und musste sehen, wie das korrespondieren könnte.

ES GIBT IN DEINER ARBEIT EINE AUFFÄLLIGE TENDENZ ZU ROMANTISCHEN BILDWELTEN, ETWA NÄCHTLICHEN MOTIVEN.

In meiner letzten Ausstellung wollte ich durch bestimmte Bilder eine stark codierte, zugespitzte Vorstellung des exotisch Anderen in den Raum einbringen. Also Aufnahmen nackter japanischer Jungen und astronomische Fotografien aus einem ebenfalls sehr zurückgenommenen Buch aus den 1960er Jahren. Allein durch die Auswahl dieser beiden Bücher und das Überblenden der Bilder der *Naked Festivals* in Japan, diesem großartigen Bacchanal, mit den Fotos des Universums wird die Orientierung erschwert. Man fragt sich, wo und wie das sein kann und wird auf die Unfähigkeit der Technik verwiesen, das Reale zu realisieren. Es war eine romantische Geste, diese Fotos ineinander zu blenden.

UND DAS UNIVERSUM ERWIES SICH DABEI ALS „DÜNN WIE PAPIER".

Es ging darum, sich durch das Papier hindurch in Richtung einer anderen Punktierung zu bewegen. *The sky is thin as paper here* ist auch ein Burroughs-Zitat. Irgendwann in den 1830er Jahre auf einem Friedhof in Boulder, Colorado, feuert eine Gruppe von Cowboys zufällig eine Pistole ab und dabei schießen sie ein Loch in den Himmel. So erkennen sie, dass ihre Wirklichkeit eigentlich etwas Fabriziertes ist und dass sie sich mitten auf einer Bühne befinden.

DU ERZEUGST ATMOSPHÄREN, DIE ENTSCHLOSSEN REDUZIERT SIND UND EIGENARTIG GLÄSERN, FAST KUBRICK-ARTIG ELEGANT WIRKEN.

Wenn man Arbeiten in einen Raum stellt, dann beginnen sie zu performen und laden sich auf. Aber das ist für mich nie eine klare und einfache Angelegenheit. Es ist vielmehr der vorschnelle Verschluss, dem ich mich zu widersetzen versuche.

DEINE ARBEIT STELLT SICH ABER IN EINER BESTIMMTEN FORM DAR UND ES IST NICHT IMMER EINFACH, SICH ÜBER ERSTE MISSVERSTÄNDNISSE HINWEGZUSETZEN. DANN FÜHLT MAN SICH STÄRKER IN DIE KLANGVOLLEN, REICH GESCHICHTETEN STRUKTUREN INVOLVIERT, WAS ABER NICHT BEDEUTET, DASS SICH DARAUS EIN EFFEKT IN HINBLICK AUF EINE INTERVIEWARTIGE SITUATION ERGIBT.

Effekt ist ein treffendes Wort. Maurice Merleau-Ponty benutzte das Wort Gelegenheit. Mich hat es immer sehr berührt, wenn ich las: Es ereignet sich in jemandem. Es ist eine elegante und außergewöhnliche Vorstellung, dass etwas in einer anderen Person zum Entstehen gebracht werden kann – eine Projektion in die Realität eines Anderen. Merleau-Ponty spricht in *Das Sichtbare und das Unsichtbare* so schön von dieser Doppelbödigkeit des Raums:

„Wie sollen wir das *Erleben des Anderen* nennen, wie es beschreiben, das ich von meinem Standort aus sehe und das mir im übrigen nicht nichts bedeutet, denn ich glaube an den Anderen – und das mich überdies auch selbst betrifft, denn es besteht dort als eine Sicht des Anderen auf mich? Vor mir dieses wohlbekannte Gesicht, sein Lächeln, die Schwankungen seiner Stimme, deren Stil mir ebenso vertraut ist wie ich mir selbst. Vielleicht beschränkt sich der Andere für mich in vielen Augenblicken meines Lebens auf jenes Schauspiel, das eine Bezauberung sein kann. Aber wenn sich die Stimme verändert, wenn etwas Ungewöhnliches auftritt in der Partitur der Dialoges oder wenn im Gegenteil eine Antwort allzu gut meinen Gedanken entspricht, ohne dass ich sie ausgesprochen hätte, – dann wird schlagartig klar, dass auch dort das Leben in jedem Augenblick erlebt wird: plötzlich schimmert irgendwo hinter diesen Augen, hinter diesen Gesten oder eher vor ihnen oder gar um sie herum, aus irgendeiner Doppelbödigkeit des Raumes heraus, durch das Gewebe meiner eigenen Welt eine andere Privatwelt hervor, und für einen Augenblick lebe ich ganz in ihr und bestehe nur noch aus der Erwiderung auf diese an mich gerichtete Aufforderung. Gewiss, schon die geringste neue Aufmerksamkeit überzeugt mich davon, dass dieser Andere, der mich vereinnahmt, bloß aus meinem Stoff gemacht ist: wie könnte ich *seine* Farben, *seinen* Schmerz, *seine* Welt überhaupt als die *seinigen* erfassen, wenn nicht aufgrund der Farben, die ich sehe, aufgrund meiner eigenen Schmerzen, aufgrund der Welt, in der ich lebe? Zumindest hat meine Privatwelt dadurch aufgehört, nur meine eigene zu sein, und sie ist fortan das Instrument, auf dem ein anderer spielt, die Dimension eines generalisierten Lebens, das meinem eigenen aufgepfropft ist."[04]

Das ist ein erstaunlicher Text, und er stammt aus seinem letzten und unvollendeten Buch, das am Ende fast ins Nichts verschwindet. Der Text zersetzt sich buchstäblich. Merleau-Ponty beginnt bei einem phänomenologischen Realen des Körpers im Raum und kommt so zu einem Punkt, an dem eine Verbindung zwischen den Menschen tatsächlich möglich wäre. Etwas später schreibt er dann:

„Es gibt einen Zirkel von Berührtem und Berührendem, das Berührte erfasst den Berührenden; es gibt einen Zirkel von Sichtbarem und Sehendem, der Sehende ist nicht ohne sichtbare Existenz; es gibt sogar die Einschreibung des Berührenden in das Sichtbare, des Sehenden in das Berührbare, und umgekehrt gibt es schließlich eine Ausbreitung des Austauschs auf alle Körper desselben Typus und Stils, die ich sehe und berühre, – und dies geschieht durch die grundlegende Spaltung oder Scheidung von Empfindendem und Empfundenem, die die Organe meines Leibes lateral miteinander kommunizieren lässt und die Transitivität von einem Leib zum anderen begründet."[05]

In dieser Idee verschmilzt die Transitivität zwischen Körpern, Ethnien und Stilen zu einem grundlegenden Konzept von Andersheit. Ich glaube, dass es in meiner Arbeit um diese sehr entwickelte, hochgradig optimistische und fast utopische Form der Übereinstimmung zwischen Menschen geht.

ÜBERSETZUNG: MANFRED HERMES

[04] MAURICE MERLEAU-PONTY: *DAS SICHTBARE UND DAS UNSICHTBARE*, HRSG. VON CLAUDE LEFORT, MÜNCHEN 1986, S. 26F.

[05] EBD., S. 187F.

BIOGRAPHY / BIOGRAFIE

1958   born at Llanelli / Wales, lives in London
                   geboren in Llanelli / Wales, lebt in London

1980   Graduated, St Martin's School of Art, London

1984   MA, Film and Video, Royal College of Art, London

SOLO EXHIBITIONS AND FILM SCREENINGS / EINZELAUSSTELLUNGEN UND FILMVORFÜHRUNGEN

2004 „Cerith Wyn Evans", Frankfurter Kunstverein, Frankfurt am Main
The sky is thin as paper here…, Galerie Daniel Buchholz, Cologne
Meanwhile Across Town, Centre Point, London
Rabbit's Moon, Camden Arts Centre, London
Museum of Fine Arts, Boston
MIT List Visual Arts Center, Boston

2003 *Look at that Picture…How does it appear to you now? Does it seem to be Persisting?*, White Cube, London
Galerie Neu, Berlin
mini Matrix, Berkeley Art Museum, San Fransisco

2002 Galerie Daniel Buchholz, Cologne (film program)

2001 Institute of Visual Culture, Kings College Chapel, London
Galerie Daniel Buchholz, Cologne
The Art Newspaper Project, Venice Biennale
Kunsthaus Glarus
Has the film already started?, Georg Kargl, Vienna

2000 *Cleave 00, Art Now*, Tate Britain, London
fig-1, Soho, London
Galerie Neu, Berlin

1999 Asprey Jacques Contemporary Art Exhibitions, London

1998 The British School at Rome in collaboration with Asprey Jacques Contemporary Art Exhibitions, Rome
Centre for Contemporary Art, Kitakyushu, Japan

1997 Deitch Projects, New York

1996 *Inverse Reverse Perverse*, White Cube/Jay Jopling, London
Studio Casa Grande, Rome

1993 *Les Visiteurs du Soir*, London Film Festival

1992 *Crossoverworkshop*, HFAK, Vienna

1990 *Sense and Influence*, Kijkhuis, The Hague

1989 *Solo Exhibition 79-89*, ICA Cinematheque, London

1983 *Solo Project*, London Film Makers Co-op

1982 *Solo Project*, Film excerpts shown on Riverside, BBC2

1981 *Solo Project*, London Film Makers Co-op
A Certain Sensibility, ICA Cinematheque, London

1980 *...And Then I „Woke Up"*, London Film Makers Co-op

SELECTED GROUP EXHIBITIONS AND FILM SCREENINGS / GRUPPENAUSSTELLUNGEN UND FILMVORFÜHRUNGEN

2004 *Welsh Venice Tour*, Glynn Vivian Art Gallery, Swansea
Sans Soleil, Galerie Neu, Berlin
Teil 2: „Quodlibet", Galerie Daniel Buchholz, Cologne

2003 Galleria Lorcan O'Neill, Rome
Only Connect, Barbican Art Gallery, London
Someone to Share My Life With, The Approach, London
The straight or crooked way, Royal College of Art Galleries, London

2002 Louis Barragan House, Mexico City
ForwArt, Palais des Beaux Arts, Hall Horta, Brussels
Lost Past / 2002-1914, various locations including Merghelynck Museum, Ypres, Belgium
Documenta 11, Kassel
My Head is on Fire but my Heart is Full of Love, Charlottenbourg Udstillingsbygning, Copenhagen
Iconoclash, ZKM, Karlsruhe
In the Freud Museum, Freud Museum, London
Screen Memories, Contemporary Art Centre, Art Tower Mito, Tokyo
Mirror: It's Only Words, London College of Printing, The London Institute, London
Void Archive, CCA, Kitakyushu, Japan
Shine, The Lowry Centre, Manchester

2001 *Diesseits und jenseits des Traums*, Sigmund Freud Museum, Vienna
What's Wrong, Trade Apartment, London
The Stunt / The Queel, London Institute, RAMC, London
Zusammenhänge im Biotop Kunst, Kunsthaus Muertz, Austria
Anthony Wilkinson Gallery, London (video screening)
Dedalic Convention, MAK, Vienna

Bridge the Gap, CCA, Kitakyushu, Japan
Gymnasion, Bregenzer Kunstverein, Bregenz
My Generation, 24 Hours of Video Art, Atlantis Gallery, London
Wir, Comawoche, Metropolis Cinema, Hamburg
Wales: Unauthorized versions, Extended Media Gallery and House of Croatian Artists, Zagreb
Yokohama Triennale of Contemporary Art, Yokohama
How do you change..., Institute of Visual Culture, Cambridge

2000 *Sensitive*, Le Printemps de Cahors, Saint-Cloud
Rumours, Arc en Reve Centre d'Architecture, Bordeaux
Ever get the feeling you've been..., A22 Projects, London
There is something you should know, Österreichische Galerie im Belvedere, Vienna
Out There, White Cube, Hoxton Square, London
The British Art Show 5, The Scottish National Gallery of Modern Art, Edinburgh
The Greenhouse Effect, Serpentine Gallery, London
Lost, Ikon Gallery, Birmingham

1999 Re Rebaudengo Gallery, Turin
54 x 54, Financial Times Building, London
Galerie Neu, Berlin
Retrace your Steps: Remember Tomorrow, Sir John Soane's Museum, London
La Ville, Le Jardin, la Mémoire, French Academy at Rome, Villa Medici, Rome
Fourth Wall, Public Art Development Trust, Royal National Theatre, London
Essential Things, Robert Prime, London

1998 *How will we behave?*, Robert Prime, London
From the Corner of the Eye, Stedelijk Museum, Amsterdam

View Four, Mary Boone, New York
Ray Rapp, Tz'Art & Co., New York
Close Echoes. Public Body and Artificial Space, City Art Gallery, Prague, and Kunsthalle Krems

1997 7th International Video Week, Geneva
Sensation, Royal Academy of Arts, London, and Hamburger Bahnhof, Berlin
A Print Portfolio from London, Atle Gerhardsen, Oslo
Gothic, ICA, London
FalseImpressions, The British School at Rome, Rome
Material Culture, Hayward Gallery, London

1996 *Sick*, 152 Brick Lane, London
Stoppage, Frac, Tours
General Release: Young British Artists, Scuola di San Pasquale, Venice
Faction Video, Royal Danish Academy of Fine Arts, Copenhagen

1995 *Life/Life*, Musée d'Art Moderne de la Ville de Paris; Centro de Exposições do Centro Cultural de Belém, Lisbon
Against, Anthony d'Offay, London
British Artists in Rome, Studio Casagrande, Rome
Faction, Focal Point Gallery, Southend

1994 *Potato*, IAS. London
Olive Tree Installation, The Orangery, Holland Park, London
Superstore Boutique, Laure Genillard Gallery, London
People Must Bed God to Stop…, Fete Worse than Death, Hoxton Square, London (Performance)
Flux, Minema Cinema, London (Film screening)
Liar, Hoxton Square, London

1993 *5th Oriel Mostyn Open Exhibition*, Oriel Mostyn, Llandudno, Wales
Modern Medicine, Barley Mow in association with Factual Nonsense Gallery, London (installation/event)

1992 *240 Minutes*, Galerie Esther Schipper, Cologne
Wooster Gardens Gallery, New York

1990 *Sign of the Times*, Museum of Modern Art, Oxford
Image and Object in Current British Art, Centre Georges Pompidou, Paris

1988 *Degrees of Blindness*, Edinburgh Film Festival
The Melancholy Imaginary, London Film Makers Co-op

1987 *The Elusive Sign*, Tate Gallery, London

1985 *Synchronisation of the Senses*, ICA Cinematheque, London
The New Pluralism, Tate Gallery, London

1984 *The Salon of the 1984*, ICA Gallery, London
Artist as Film Maker, National Film Theatre, London

1983 *The New Art*, Tate Gallery, London

1982 *Riverside – Film excerpts*, BBC2 Television, London

PHOTOCREDITS

Stephen White (23)
Andrea Stappert (95, 97, 99, 102, 103, 104, 105, 106)
Jürgen Schmidt (137, 141, 142, 143, 144)

ACKNOWLEDGMENTS / DANK AN

Nicolaus Schafhausen, Vanessa Joan Müller, Christopher Müller, Daniel Buchholz, Irene Bradbury, Natalie Lazarus, Annushka Shani, Jay Jopling and all at White Cube, Juliette Blightman, Katja Schroeder, René Zechlin, Adrian Hermanides, Frein Jäger, Michael Moos, Henrik Zimmer, Lasse Schmidt-Hansen, and all at the FKV, Georg Kargl, Alexander Schröder, Thilo Wermke, Hans Ulrich Obrist, Molly Nesbit, David Bussel, Michael Neff, Wolfgang Tillmans, Daniel Birnbaum and all at the Städelschule, The King George, Mike Smith Studio, David Cunningham, Liam Gillick, Andrea Stappert, Karl Orton, the authors, Julie Ault, and all the lenders.